The History of the English Language, 2nd Edition
Part II

Professor Seth Lerer

THE TEACHING COMPANY ®

PUBLISHED BY:

THE TEACHING COMPANY
4151 Lafayette Center Drive, Suite 100
Chantilly, Virginia 20151-1232
1-800-TEACH-12
Fax—703-378-3819
www.teach12.com

ISBN 1-59803-403-5

Seth Lerer, Ph.D.

Avalon Foundation Professor in Humanities and Professor of English
and Comparative Literature, Stanford University

Seth Lerer is the Avalon Foundation Professor in Humanities and Professor of English and Comparative Literature at Stanford University. He holds degrees from Wesleyan University (B.A., 1976), Oxford University (B.A., 1978), and the University of Chicago (Ph.D., 1981), and he taught at Princeton University from 1981 to 1990, when he moved to Stanford. Dr. Lerer has published 10 books, including *Chaucer and His Readers* (Princeton University Press, 1993) and *Inventing English: A Portable History of the Language* (Columbia University Press, 2007), and he is the author of more than 100 scholarly articles and reviews.

Professor Lerer has received many awards for his scholarship and teaching, including fellowships from the National Endowment for the Humanities and the Guggenheim Foundation, the Beatrice White Prize of the English Association of Great Britain, the Harry Levin Prize of the American Comparative Literature Association, and the Hoagland Prize for undergraduate teaching at Stanford.

Table of Contents
The History of the English Language, 2nd Edition
Part II

The History of the English Language, 2nd Edition

Scope:

This course of 36 lectures surveys the history of the English language, from its origins as a dialect of Germanic-speaking peoples, through the literary and cultural documents of its 1,500-year span, to the state of American speech of the present day. In addition to surveying the spoken and written forms of the language over time, the course also focuses on larger social concerns about language use, variety, and change; the relationship between spelling and pronunciation; the notion of dialect and variation across geographical and class boundaries; the arguments concerning English as an official language and the status of standard English; the role of the dictionary in describing and prescribing usage; and the ways in which words change meaning, as well as the manner in which English speakers have coined and borrowed new words from other languages.

The course is in three parts. Part I focuses on the development of English in its earliest forms. We begin with the study of Indo-European, the posited 5,000-year-old original from which the modern and classical European, Iranian, and Indian languages emerged. From Indo-European, the lectures move to the Germanic branch of languages and to the Anglo-Saxons who settled the British Isles beginning in the 5th century. Old English emerges as the literary vernacular of the Anglo-Saxons and flourishes until the Norman Conquest in the mid-11th century. The interplay of English, French, and Latin from the 11th to the 15th centuries generates the forms of Middle English in which Chaucer, among others, wrote, and gives us a sense of a trilingual medieval British culture.

Part II begins with the reemergence of English as an official language after the decline of French in the 15th century. This set of lectures charts the changes in pronunciation, grammar, and vocabulary that distinguish Middle English from Modern English (in particular, the Great Vowel Shift). It looks closely at the rise of an English literary vernacular, especially in Shakespeare, Milton, the King James Bible, and the dictionary of Samuel Johnson, and it suggests some ways in which we can trace changes in word meanings by using the resources of historical dictionaries.

Part III focuses on American English and the modes of studying the history of the language today. The lectures explore the rise of American dialects, differences between American and British pronunciation and usage, and the emergence of distinctive American voices in literature, social criticism, and politics. The languages of African-Americans and the place of English as a world language texture our appreciation of the varieties of what English has become, and the course concludes with some provocations on the scientific study of language, the rise of linguistics as an academic discipline, and the possible future of English in society.

Lecture Thirteen
The Return of English as a Standard

Scope:

This lecture surveys the history of English from the late 14th to the early 16th centuries, to illustrate the ways in which political and social attitudes returned it to the status of the prestige vernacular (over French). It also looks at some of the important institutions—the court, the law, and commerce, in particular—that helped effect the return of English as a standard. Finally, this lecture examines some attitudes of the time toward the status of English in relationship to French, and toward the question of English regional dialects. The importation of the printing press by William Caxton in the 1470s had a significant effect on what kind of English came to be read and written and, in turn, what the relationships were between literary English and "official" English.

Outline

I. As we've seen, throughout the Middle Ages, there were three languages used in the British Isles, with Latin and French as the prestige languages of court and culture, education, and economy. During the late 14th and early 15th centuries, however, English seemed to return as a prestige language.

   A. In this and the next few lectures, we will discuss how English reasserted itself after the decline of French in the late Middle Ages, and what is different about English in its reemergence.

   B. We'll also chart some changes from the English of Chaucer to the time of Shakespeare, and we'll explore in detail how Modern English finally emerged.

II. English did not, of course, disappear after the Norman Conquest. Even though French became the official language of court and commerce and Latin was used in the church and university, English remained the vehicle for imaginative expression. How did it return as the language of official proclamation, economic control, and political and social order?

A. The first "official" use of English after the conquest was in the proclamation of Henry III from 18 October 1258, in which he swears to observe the dictates of the Magna Carta (1215).

   1. This document was also issued in French and Latin. What is interesting is not just that Henry felt the need to prepare a text in English, but that the English text is obviously a translation of the French one. French was Henry's language and still the official language of the court.

   2. A comparison of the French and Middle English versions of the document reveals that the translators deliberately used archaic-sounding English words and phrases for political effect.

B. Parliament was not addressed in English until 1362, and even after that time, the records of speeches were still kept in French.

   1. We know that some people spoke in English because certain speeches were introduced in the *Rotuli Parlementorum* (*The Rolls of Parliament*) with the phrase *Monstre en Englois*, "announced in English."

   2. We don't know whether transcriptions of the speeches were made in English and then translated to French, or whether the scribes were bilingual and were able to take dictation in French while English was being spoken.

C. At the end of the 14th century and the beginning of the 15th, English came to predominate as the official language of record.

   1. By 1423, Parliament's records were kept virtually all in English.

   2. Henry V (r. 1413–1422) established English as an official language.

   3. Statutes (laws based on petitions) were in the following languages: in Latin to 1300; in French until 1485; in English and French from 1485 to 1489; and solely in English after 1489.

   4. The London Brewer's Guild adopted English as its official language of record in 1422.

5. In 1397, the Earl of Kent made what we believe was the first major noble English will after the Norman Conquest. In 1438, the Countess of Stafford made her will in English. The wills of kings Henry IV, Henry V, and Henry VI were all in English.

6. Shakespeare went so far as to present Henry V as not even conversant in French, an example of the rewriting of history.

7. Some critics argue that Chaucer's revival in the 15th century was itself the product of a nationalistic movement.

D. As the prestige of English rose, French underwent a decline.

1. By the early 1490s, the printer William Caxton (c. 1430–1492) could write that the greatest number of people in the realm of England understood neither Latin nor French.

2. There is a growing body of evidence that by the end of the 15th century, French became less and less the language of culture and social prestige.

III. A standard form of English accompanied the rise of the institution known as "Chancery."

A. *Chancery* comes from the word *chancel*, or chapel of the king, where the chaplains of the court originally spent their time between services, writing the king's letters.

B. By the end of the 14th century, Chancery was the production house for official government documents. By the mid-15th century, the term came to refer to the national bureaucracy as a whole (except for the Exchequer, the economic side of administration).

C. Chancery established special forms of spelling and handwriting that were taught to scribes for the production of official documents. William Caxton opened his print shop in Westminster, the site of Chancery and the administrative seat of government, to establish the idea that his documents were printed in "official" English (Chancery English).

D. Chancery English contributed to the development of a form of writing that was a standard, irrespective of the speech or dialect of the writer.

1. Spelling was standardized without regard for pronunciation.
2. The official language ceased to represent any living spoken dialect.
3. Writing became truly conventional and arbitrary.
4. Chancery was the first standard of writing in the vernacular in England since Aethelwold's school at Winchester 400 or so years before.

   E. Chancery English survives for us today in a set of petitions, such as the one from the royal orator William Walsby written to King Henry VI in 1437, asking to be appointed Dean of Hastings Cathedral.

1. In this petition, we see that some spellings, such as those of *benign* and *said*, were regularized regardless of dialect.
2. We also see the emergence of *you* and *your* as the standard second-person pronoun forms, as opposed to the earlier use of two sets of pronouns (informal and singular: *thee, thou, thine*; formal and plural: *ye, you, your*).

IV. By using Chancery English, William Caxton established a national literary standard in print based on the written standard of official documentation. This was a radical change in the notion of a standard and in the standard's relationship to regional dialect and official forms.

   A. Let us review several myths that surround the early history of printing.

1. Printing did not create or increase national literacy overnight.
2. Printing did not democratize literacy across class boundaries. Early printed books were expensive, did not appear in large quantities, and were designed for a readership of clerks and gentlemen.
3. Printed books at first looked no different from manuscripts; the typefaces were based on handwriting.

   B. Printing did, however, foster the rise of Chancery standard English.

1. Because Caxton based his press in Westminster and because he established himself as a printer with royal,

aristocratic, and "gentle" patrons, his work had an official cast.

2. Caxton exhibited a self-consciousness about the kind of language that should be standard and, as we said, adapted the standard of official government writing to the printing of literary texts.

C. Caxton was aware of the problems associated with standards, which he discussed in a preface to his book *Eneydos*, a translation into English of a French version of Virgil's *Aenid* (1490). Here, he reflects on attitudes toward language change, dialect variation, and the arbitration of English usage by the educated and the elite.

1. Caxton relates a story in which a merchant from London knocks on the door of a Kentish farm and asks for eggs. The farm wife who answers the door doesn't understand the merchant's request for *eggs* (the Northern or Scandinavian form of the word) rather than *eyren* (the Old English and Southern form) and tells him that she doesn't speak French.

2. *"What sholde a man in thyse dayes now wryte, egges or eyren?"* asks Caxton. *"It is harde to playse euery man by cause of dyersite and change of language."*

3. Caxton's preface is an allegory of linguistic alienation that reminds us of St. Augustine and other earlier commentators. The English language has become so mutable and diverse that it is not only Northern barbarians but Kentish housewives, as well, who cannot understand what a Londoner is saying.

4. At the same time, Caxton reflects on the relationship between language and the self. What is the English language? What makes someone "English"? Is a merchant from London any more or less "English" than a housewife from Kent?

Reading:

Albert C. Baugh and Thomas Cable, *A History of the English Language*.

John Hurt Fisher, *The Emergence of Standard English*.

John Hurt Fisher, et al., *An Anthology of Chancery English*.

Questions to Consider:

1. Why was English so slow to be adopted as the official language of England after the Norman Conquest?

2. Did the rise of Chancery make English a more powerful language?

Lecture Thirteen—Transcript
The Return of English as a Standard

English makes a comeback. Throughout the Middle Ages, as I had discussed in my previous lectures, the British Isles was a trilingual country—that is, English, French, and Latin. For centuries, Latin and French were the prestige languages of court and culture, education and economy.

During the late 14th and early 15th centuries, however, English seems to return as a prestige language. What I would like to do in this lecture and in the next few lectures will be to talk about how English reasserts itself after the decline of French in the late Middle Ages, and what is different about the English that reemerges as a prestige language in England in the 15th and 16th centuries.

I'm going to talk about how we can chart changes from the English of Chaucer to the time of Shakespeare, and in this lecture and in the next few lectures, I'm going to be looking in detail at how Modern English, the English that we can recognize in sound and spelling and in sense today, how that Modern English finally emerged.

Of course, English had not disappeared after the Norman Conquest, for even though French was the language of court and commerce, and Latin was the language of church and school and university learning, English remained, as we have seen, as the language of imaginative expression. It was the language of the street; it was the language also of the poem. A whole range of English verse and prose survives from the 12th, 13th, and 14th centuries to testify to the vitality of the vernacular during this period.

But during this period English is not, as it were, an "official" language. And so one of the interesting questions we need to ask is how English returns as a language of official proclamation, of economic control, and of political and social order.

You'll remember that the Norman Conquest was in 1066. The first official use of English after the Conquest was not until almost two full centuries later. This is a proclamation of King Henry III, that was issued in October of 1258—18 October, 1258. The document was issued in French and in Latin and in English. The idea of this document is that King Henry swears to observe the dictates of

Magna Carta. Magna Carta was that great document that had been signed by King John in 1215.

Henry had never kept his word on this, and the proclamation was designed to assure the barons that he would respect the order of political control that had been established in the Magna Carta. The fact that the document is issued in three languages suggests that business was going on in three languages, but I think that there's something else at work here.

A close reading of this document—and I'm going to look just at the opening of it—has shown to many scholars that, in fact, the document was originally written in French—that French for the 1250s, for Henry III, was the official language; it was Henry's own language. But there is an effort, or if you like, a rhetorical gesture towards the English barons and towards the realm of England as a whole, to have the document in English. So my point is that the publication or the presentation of this English document is less about language than it is about politics.

Let me read to you the opening phrases of this document:

> *Henri, par le grace Deu, Rey de Engleterre, sire de Irlande, duc de Normandie, de Aquitien, et conte de Angou, a tuz sez feaus clers et lays saluz.*

In Middle English, that reads:

> *Henri, þurȝ Godes fultume King on Engleneloande, Lhoaverd on Yrloande, Duk on Normandi, on Aquitaine, and Eorl on Anjow, send i-gretinge to alle hise holde, i-lærde and i-leawede on Huntendone-shire.*

This is fascinating because it's quite clear that at a certain level, what the English scribes and translators are trying to do is come up with English versions of the French. *Par le grace Deu* (*By God's grace*). Now that is a Frenchism; it is a Gallic expression—by the grace of God. *Grace Deu* (*the grace of God*).

What the English translator does is translates it into the words *Godes fultume*. The word *ful* has as its root "fullness" or completion. It passes into Middle English, but it seems clear that by the 13th century this is a very antique or archaic word. In fact, according to the dictionaries of English, this document of 1258 is the last recorded use of the word *fultume*.

There are many examples like this, and the point to make is this, that what has been going on here is that this French text is translated into a deliberately archaic-sounding English—that is, that it is being translated into an English that sounds old and also an English that is deliberately purged of newer phrases. So when Henri greets all of his clerks and all of his laymen in French—*les clers* (*the clerks*); *et lays* (*and the laymen*)—in the English it is phrased as an Old English alliterative pair: "*i-lærde*" and "*i-leawede*", (*the learned* and *the lewd*). *Lewd* here means uneducated.

What I'm suggesting here is this: that our documents from early English history are not simply documents of language, but they are documents of politics; that archaism can be used for special political effect; and that when we see translations and when we see this trilingual or multilingual world going on in medieval England, we have to be extremely careful about what the language is signaling.

Parliament was not addressed in English until almost another century later. And in 1362, Parliament is opened for the first time with a speech in English. Now the problem is this: that the records of that speech are in French. The so-called records of Parliament are the *Rotuli Parlementorum*—that is, *The Rolls of Parliament*, because they were kept on large rolls of parchment. If we read the entry for 1362 for the opening of Parliament we're told that, "*Au quell jour,*" (on this day) "*esteanz nostre Seigneur le Roi ...*" (in the presence of our King). And it goes on.

In the presence of our King and the counts and the barons and the privy counselors and everyone else, the Chief Justice, *Chef Justice le Roi,* summoned Parliament. "*Monstre en Englois.*"

That is, he announced in English the following thing, but it's recorded for us in French. I find this another fascinating document because what I want to ask is this: What's going on here? Is this a text that's being translated from an English transcription? In other words, do you have scribes in Parliament who are taking dictation, and they're taking dictation in English? Then when the time comes to record it officially, it's recorded officially in French? That's option number one.

Option number two, which I actually prefer to believe, is that all of the transcription was going on in French. In other words, that what you have is a case of simultaneous translation and the trained scribes are bilingual. They are writing it down and translating it into French as it is being spoken in English. French is the language of written legal record.

So what happens at the end of the 14th and the beginning of the 15th century, English comes to predominate as not just the language of court or culture or commerce, but as the official language of record. Let me give you some dates now. By 1423, Parliament's records were kept virtually all in English.

King Henry V, who reigned from 1413 to 1422, established English as an official language. It is fair to say that he is the first English king for whom the idea of a "King's English" exists. Statutes—that is, laws that were based on petitions—are in the following languages: to 1300, they're in Latin; until 1485, they're in French; in English and French until 1485–1489; and then after 1489, they are solely kept in English.

What we're looking at is really a century of transition. What's going on in commerce? The London Brewer's Guild—that is, the group responsible for the brewing and the distribution of beer in London, which was an extremely important guild in Medieval England—they adopted English as its official language in a record of 1422.

Let's look at wills. The first, as far as we can tell, major noble English will after the Conquest is the 1397 will of the Earl of Kent. In 1438, the Countess of Stafford made her will in English, and the wills of kings Henry IV, Henry V, and Henry VI are all in English. Now it is true that these documents are in English, but it is also true that French remained still the prestige language of the court.

If you know Shakespeare's play *Henry V*, what Shakespeare does there is he rewrites history by reinforcing Henry's role as master of the King's English. Henry, the victor of the Battle of Agincourt; Henry the wooer of the French princess. He makes Henry monolingual in English, which certainly would not have been the case, but he wants to rewrite history; he wants to rewrite linguistic history to suggest that.

Some critics have also argued that there was a revival of the works of Geoffrey Chaucer. You'll remember from my previous lecture that Chaucer was writing in the 1380s and 1390s. He died in 1400. There is no manuscript—that is, there is no document of Chaucer's poetry from his own lifetime. There's nothing in his own hand, and there's no datable text to the 14th century.

Manuscripts of Chaucer's work do not appear until the first two decades of the 15th century. One reason for this may well have been that with the revival of English as an official language, certain circles in English courts and aristocratic culture wanted a poet in English to match, as it were, a king in English. So Chaucer's poetry was rediscovered and recopied. So Chaucer becomes, in effect, an English poet for an England after his own time.

What we're looking at here is a new rise of official English. And as that English rises, French is undergoing a decline. William Caxton was England's first printer, and he was born sometime around 1430 and he died probably in about 1491 or 1492. In works published—that is, printed by him in England in 1490 and 1491—Caxton has prologues or prefaces. In one of them, he writes that, "The greatest number of people in the realm of England no longer understand either Latin or French."

So it's quite clear that by the end of the 15th century, French is beginning to decline as a prestige language. This statement suggests that these languages are no longer the languages of culture and social prestige. So one question is when Caxton sets up his print shop, what is going to be the form of language he's going to use to print English literature and to print official English? At this point, I want to turn to an institutional development that had a great impact on the crystallization of late Middle English and the return of English as an official language.

This institution is known as Chancery. *Chancery* is a word that comes from the word *chancel*, or chapel of the king. This is where the chaplains of the court originally spent their time between services writing the king's letters. By the end of the 14th century, Chancery came to be the place where official documents were produced. By the mid-15th century, the term came to refer to the national bureaucracy as a whole, except for the Exchequer—that is, the economic side of administration.

What Chancery was, it was a kind of—now remember, this is before print, so we're producing handwritten documents—it's a kind of combination of official government printing house—well, they're not printing—government document house; a kind of official place of dissemination of government documents, a secretariat of state and also a school. Scribes would be coming *from every shires ende*, to quote Chaucer again. From all over England, young men were coming to London to make their way, and the smart and the literate ones could enter Chancery and they could be taught in Chancery schools how to read and write, and how to produce those documents.

What Chancery did was it established a very special form of spelling and a very special form of handwriting—an idiom of language that was used for these official documents. Caxton set up his print shop in Westminster which was a city then; now it's part of London, but Westminster was a separate entity then. The city of London in the Middle Ages, is what we now call "the City"—that is, the financial center—the old area of the Tower, the East End. That was the city of London, but Westminster was the administrative seat of government.

By setting up his print shop there, Caxton makes the point that he is going to be printing in a language of official English. Chancery was official English. So what happens here is that you have a system of writing, of spelling, of letter formation, and of organization that was a standard irrespective of the speech or the dialect of the writer. What matters is not the usage of an individual scribe. What matters is, if you like, the institutional or official set of uses; and royal clerks were writing almost exclusively in English after 1417.

Let's look at some details of Chancery English. Chancery English developed a form of writing that was standard, irrespective of pronunciation. Spelling was a convention. The official language ceased to represent any living spoken dialect. Writing became truly conventional and arbitrary, and this was the first standard of writing the vernacular in England, probably since Aelthelwold's school at Winchester 400 years before.

I want to just give you a little taste of Chancery English. Chancery English survives for us in a set of documents, or in a set of petitions, and here is a little bit of one. I'm going to read you just a little bit and talk about it to analyze this Chancery language.

> *Please it to the Kyng oure souerain Lord of youre Benigne*
> *grace to graunte to youre humble servant and Oratoure sir*
> *William Walsby Tresorer with the Quene youre moder the*
> *denerye of hastynges in the dyose of Chichester the which*
> *Prestewyke Clerke of youre parlement late had on who soule*
> *god assolle And youre saide Oratour shal pray god for you.*

Now I've read this in modern pronunciation, but I want to call attention to some key things about spelling. It should be very clear to you what's going on. This is a plea from William Walsby, a courtier. He is the royal orator and he's writing to Henry VI in the year 1437. He's asking for a favor. What he's asking to be is Dean of Hastings Cathedral in the diocese of Chichester. It's submitted—it's dated—the 8th day of November, in the 15th year of the reign of Henry VI, and that's 1437.

What's very interesting about this document from the point of view of scholarship is the way in which spellings are being regularized, regardless of dialect. So words like *benign* are spelled B-E-N-I-G-N, and this is a spelling convention—that is, the scribes are using this "-gn" to signal that the vowel before it is long. The word *said* is being written S-A-I-D and standardized, whereas in Middle English it would have been written S-E-I-D, S-A-I-D, or S-E-I-D-E.

There are many other conventions that are operating as well here, and one of the primary conventions, I think, in Chancery English as well, is the way in which the "*you*" and the "*your*" forms become the standard second person forms. In other words, you'll remember from my earlier lecture that Old, Middle, and early Modern English, as all of the modern European languages, had informal and singular forms of the second person pronoun—*thee, thou, thine*—and formal and plural ones—*you* and *your*. Informal singular, formal plural.

What's going on in Chancery is that a convention is being set up that regardless of whom you are addressing, you're going to call them *you*. This begins, if you like, to percolate through learned written English, spoken English, so that over the next 100 years, *you* becomes, if you like, the unmarked form, and *thou* becomes the marked form.

What does all of this have to do with William Caxton? What Caxton did was when he decided to print the works of English literature, he printed them in Chancery English. So when you look at, for example, his printings of Chaucer, Caxton is printing Chaucer in the 1470s and '80s. Chaucer was writing a century before. Caxton, in effect, translates or modernizes or recasts Chaucer's language into Chancery English. This is, I want to stress, a profound change—that is, a national literary standard in print is now based on a written standard of official documentation. This is a radical change in the notion of "standard" and in the notion of that standard's relationship to regional dialect and to official forms.

Caxton, as a printer, did not change things overnight. There are many myths about printing and I just want to pause to review a few of them. Printing did not create literacy overnight. Early printed books did not appear in vast quantities—they were very expensive. They were items of value, much as handwritten manuscripts were items of value. They were designed for clerks and gentlemen. In other words, printing is not about democratizing literacy; printing for Caxton is another kind of commodity, if you like. And printed books looked no different from manuscripts. The typefaces of early printed books were based on handwriting.

What printing did, however, was it fostered the rise of Chancery Standard English. In the course of this rise, because Caxton based his press in Westminster, and because he established himself as a printer with royal, aristocratic, and gentle patrons, his work has an official cast to it. And so what you see in Caxton is a self-consciousness, if you like, about the kind of language that should be standard.

Caxton adopted a standard of official writing to the printing of literary texts, and just to reiterate, he made an official standard a literary standard. Caxton was acutely aware of the problems of these standards and in the prologue to his book called the *Eneydos*—this is an English translation of a French translation of a version of Virgil's *Aeneid*, printed in 1490—in this preface, Caxton reflects on attitudes towards language change, dialect variation, the arbitration of English usage by the educated and the elite.

What Caxton reflects upon is precisely what kind of dialect and what kind of spelling should be used in the printing of official documents and English literature. One of the ways he reflects on this is he tells a little story. And here is his story. I'm going to read it in Caxton's late Middle English and translate it for you:

It happened that certain marchauntes were in a shippe in tamyse for to haue sayled ouer the see into selande and for lack of wynde, they taryed at a forlond, and wente to land to refreshe them:

So it happened that certain merchants were in a ship in the Thames River, and they were planning to sail across the channel into Zeeland—that is, to Holland and the Low Countries. But because of a lack of wind, they had to wait on the coast, and so they went to land to refresh themselves.

Here are London merchants and they're going onto land, and this is Kent. You will remember the Kentish dialect of Middle English was very distinctive. So Caxton goes on:

One of theym … cam in to an hows and axed for mete: and specially he axed after eggys;

He asked for food. The Middle English word for food is *mete*. What it says is he asked for something to eat, and in particular, he asked for eggs.

And the goode wife, answered, that she coude speke no frenshe.

And the good woman of the house answered that she could speak no French.

And the marchaunt was angry, for he also coude speke no frenshe, but wolde have egges and she vnderstode hym not.

And the merchant was angry because he also could speak no French, but he wanted eggs, and she didn't understand him.

And than at laste a nother sayd that he wolde haue eyre, and the good wyf sayd that she vnderstod him wel.

And then another man said that what he wanted was *eyre*, and the good wife said she understood him clearly.

Eggs is a Northern form. The Old English and Southern form of the noun meaning the thing that a chicken lays is *eyre*—*eyre* or *eyren* in the Old English plural. The Northern or Scandinavian form is *egg* and *egges*. You will remember that the Scandinavian languages and Northern English had those "guh" sounds—*muggy, ugly*—that were very distinctive.

What happened was that by the end of the 15th century, Northerners coming into London, working in Chancery, the Inns of Court, going to the universities—people who were in effect the descendants of the kind of clerks that Chaucer parodied in "The Reeve's Tale"—parts of their dialect were absorbed into the metropolitan standard. One part of the Northern dialect that was absorbed into the metropolitan standard was the word for eggs.

So here is this educated London merchant, and one imagines him, you know, with his hat and with his cloak coming in from the ship and knocking on a farmhouse door and he asks for eggs, and the wife says, "I don't speak French." So he's very angry because he couldn't speak French either. The point is that in Kent, it's still the old Southern and Old English form *eyren*.

What Caxton then goes on to say is:

> *What sholde a man in thyse dayes now wryte,*

> What should a man write these days,

> *egges or eyren? It is harde to playse euery man by cause of dyuersite & chaunge of langage.*

> It's hard to please every man because of diversity and change and language.

What Caxton is doing is he is recognizing that English is historically and dialectically diverse, and that as a printer—as a printer of official documents, as a printer of English literature, as a printer based in Westminster—Caxton must decide what forms of English to use, and those forms, in effect, will become a standard. But there is a philosophical question as well, and there's something wonderful about this story that has the feel of a medieval romance about it.

Now go back to St. Augustine; go back to the Middle Ages; go back to those theologians—"man is a grammatical animal." "We live in a land of unlikeliness." "The diversity of languages alienates man from man." Recall John of Trevisa and the *scharp, slyttyng* and *frotyng* and *unschape* sounds of the North.

What Caxton has given us is a little allegory of linguistic alienation. We come upon a landscape now, not of Northern barbarians, but of Kentish housewives who cannot understand what we are saying, for the English language is so mutable and so diverse that we live in a Babel—in a fallen world. Just before he tells this story, Caxton says:

> We Englishmen [and now I'm just going to translate] are born under the control of the moon which is never the same, but is always wavering—waxing at one time, waning and decreasing at another time, and the common English that is spoken in one county varies from that of another.

So what Caxton reflects on at the end of the 15th century is he reflects on diversity and alienation, but he's also reflecting on the relationship between English and the self. What is the "English" language now? What makes someone "English?" Is a merchant from London any more or less English than a housewife from Kent?

In my subsequent lectures, I'm going to be showing how the changes in pronunciation, in vocabulary, and in grammar were happening so quickly in the late 15th and 16th centuries that many people were asking what English might be and were lamenting the fact that living in this sublunary world we find ourselves alienated from the tongues we speak.

Lecture Fourteen
The Great Vowel Shift and Modern English

Scope:

In this lecture, we will look at the major features of the Great Vowel Shift (GVS), a systematic change in the pronunciation of long, stressed vowels in English. The shift took place from about the middle of the 15th century and continued until about the end of the 16th. It changed radically the sound of spoken English, making its vowels unique in pronunciation among European languages. It also had an impact on attitudes toward dialect and usage, and it affected the way in which English verse was written (by changing radically the rhyming possibilities of the language). Finally, it was the key change in the language that transformed Middle English into Modern English. This lecture, therefore, marks that important transition. Study of the GVS also gives us a glimpse at some of the methods by which scholars understand language change. In particular, we can look at written documents whose unsure spelling gives us evidence for the GVS as it was happening.

Outline

I. The Great Vowel Shift (GVS) was a relatively simple phenomenon, but it had a significant impact on the sound and shape of the English language between the time of Chaucer and the time of Shakespeare.

   A. Indeed, it is because of the GVS that the language of Chaucer was largely opaque by Shakespeare's time. Shakespeare's language, in contrast, is still accessible to us because no change in pronunciation as systematic or as radical as the GVS has taken place since his time.

   B. During the period of the GVS, from roughly the middle of the 15th century to the end of the 16th century, changes in vocabulary and word meanings, syntax, and attitudes toward language use, regional variation, and public idiom took place in English. Together with the change in pronunciation effected by the GVS, these features of the language transformed Middle English into Early Modern English.

C. In this lecture, we'll work through the details of the sound changes that took place during the GVS and look at the ways in which scholars are able to use written documents to provide evidence for changes in sound. We'll also see how the GVS has become something of a myth in English linguistic history.

II. The GVS signals the single most important change from Middle to Modern English, and it separates English from other European languages.

A. Only six vowels were affected. These are long, stressed monophthongs—vowels in stressed positions in the word that were held long in pronunciation and that had a pure sound (that is, were not made up of groups of sounds).

1. A monophthong is a single sound made by keeping the mouth in the same position. Examples include /ɛ/ ("eh" as in *bet*), /i/ ("ee"), /o/ ("oh"), /u/ ("oo"), and /ɔ/ ("aah" as in *mop*).

2. In speaking these sounds, the mouth stays in the same position. In contrast, "I" is a diphthong, a sound made up of two sounds, and when this sound is spoken, the mouth moves from one position to another. Examples include the "i" sound in *mice* and the "au" sound in *house*.

B. The sounds affected by the GVS are shown in the following table.

Sound	Written Representation	Example Word and Middle English Pronunciation
/a/	a-	name, "nahme"
/e/	e-	feet, "fayt-eh"
/i/	i-	bite, "beet-eh"
/o/	o-	do, "dough"
/u/	u-	mus, "moose"
/ai/	i-	myn "mine"

C. The GVS can be described in terms of articulatory phonetics; as you may recall from one of our early lectures, articulatory phonetics is used to describe how vowels and consonants are produced in the mouth. Vowels are described according to their height and their position in the mouth. Thus, they can be low, middle, or high, and back, mid, or front.

1. Keep in mind that linguists do not use the terms "long" and "short" to describe a qualitative difference in vowel sound, as most people are taught in school (e.g., *beet* versus *bit*). From a linguistic point of view, the terms "long" and "short" relate to quantitative vowel length, that is, the period of time through which the vowel sound is held. This length of time made a difference in meaning in Old and Middle English.

2. For example, in Old English, the word *god* could be pronounced "gode," meaning *God*, or "gooade," meaning *good*. The length of time the vowel was held signaled a different meaning for the word.

3. This distinction was lost to Modern English during the GVS. There is no difference in meaning if *sat* is pronounced "sat" or "saat."

D. The GVS can be summarized as follows:

1. Front vowels were raised and fronted.
2. Back vowels were raised and retracted.
3. High vowels were made into diphthongs.

E. The following represents a scholarly reconstruction of the changes.

1. The two high front vowels represented by the letters "i-" (/i/, pronounced "ee") and "u-" (/u/, pronounced "oo") in Middle English became diphthongs. In other words, they were pronounced differently, each as a cluster of two sounds: /i/ became /ai/, pronounced "I", and /u/ became /au/, pronounced "ow."

   a. In Middle English, *mice* would have been pronounced "meese," and *house* would have been pronounced "hoose."

   b. By the end of the 16th century, these sounds probably would have been pronounced "moice" and "hause," and by the end of the 17th century, they would have been close to our modern pronunciations.

2. The mid vowels represented by the letters "e" (/e/, pronounced like the "a" in "ace") and "o" (/o/, pronounced "oh") were raised. Thus, Middle English *feet*, pronounced "fate," came to be pronounced as Modern English "feet." Middle English *do*, pronounced "dough," came to be pronounced as Modern English "do."

3. The low back vowel written in Middle English as "a" (/a/, pronounced "aw") rose to fill the place left by the older Middle English "e." Thus, a word such as *name*, pronounced in Middle English as "nahme," became pronounced "naim."

4. Finally, the long, open "o" (/ɔ/, pronounced like the "o" in *cost*) was raised to the long "o." Thus, the Middle English word *so*, pronounced "saw," came to be pronounced "so."

III. More than one explanation exists for the GVS.

    A. Dialects in England during the 15th and 16th centuries were in contact in new ways.

        1. Migrations from the north and the midlands into London brought speakers into contact.

        2. This mix of dialects created social pressures to develop or select a set of pronunciations that would have new social status or prestige.

        3. The sounds that were chosen or developed appear, in retrospect, as the sounds of the GVS.

        4. Of course, people did not consciously decide to change their pronunciation according to the GVS. There were many ways of pronouncing vowels, some regional and some historical, but over time, a particular system of pronunciation arose as an accepted standard form.

    B. An additional explanation is that, with the change in the social status in English itself and with the loss of French as the prestige language, the need was felt to fill the social gap with a new form of speech.

IV. Returning for a moment to the diphthongs, we noted that /ai/ and /au/ from /i/ and /u/ didn't become full diphthongs overnight.

    A. The word *my*, for example, would not have been pronounced as Middle English "me" but "moy"; *bite* would be "boyte";

fight would be "foyt." These interim pronunciations seem to be the origin of "pirate English."

B. In other words, we might say that pirate English is a form of the language in which the GVS hadn't fully run its course, and the high front monophthongs of Middle English hadn't fully diphthongized.

V. It's also true that the GVS had not fully run its course as late as the early 18th century.

    A. Alexander Pope, writing in the 18th century, reveals that the GVS wasn't complete, through his rhyming of such words as *join* ("joyn") and *line* ("loyn").

    B. There also survives a large body of letters from the 15th and 16th centuries, mostly family correspondence, that provides evidence of the GVS in process.

        1. In this correspondence, we see people with varying degrees of education writing to each other. Some of them used Chancery forms; some used older Middle English spellings; and some used spellings that reflected their speech habits.

        2. Old spelling conventions are often used in these letters to indicate new sounds. For example, *meet* would have been pronounced "mayt" in Middle English but is spelled *myte* or *mite* in 15th- and 16th-century writing to reflect its new pronunciation, "meet."

        3. Other examples include those in the following table. Many of these created spellings indicate changes in the vowels to diphthongs.

Example	Middle English Pronunciation	Spelling to Reflect Pronunciation after the GVS
hear	"hare"	hyre, hire
abide	"abeed"	abeyd
our	"uurr"	aur
out	"oot"	owt
house	"hoos"	hows

VI. We need to understand the GVS in tandem with the rise in the standard forms of written English being developed in Chancery and used by Caxton and his successors in print which we discussed in the last lecture.

    A. We see a growing gap between educated writing and speech. As you recall, Chancery had set up a system of spelling for official documents which could be learned by scribes regardless of their regional backgrounds. Thus, spelling was gradually becoming conventionalized and divorced from speech; it no longer represented pronunciation.

    B. An added effect of this growing separation was a change in punctuation. In the Middle Ages, punctuation was, in essence, ear punctuation—it signaled breaks in reading aloud. By Caxton's time, punctuation was moving toward eye punctuation; that is, it was designed for the silent reader, signaling syntactic or clausal units of a sentence.

VII. A small group of words spelled with "ea," such as *steak*, *great*, *break*, and *yea*, did not undergo the GVS. If they had, they would have been pronounced "steek," "greet," "breek," and "yee." As with other linguistic anomalies, we have no explanation for the fact that these words didn't change, while similar words did.

Reading:

Albert C. Baugh and Thomas Cable, *A History of the English Language*.

Matthew Giancarlo, "The Rise and Fall of the Great Vowel Shift?" in *Representations*.

Roger Lass, "Phonology and Morphology," in Roger Lass, ed., *The Cambridge History of the English Language*, Vol. 3: 1476-1776.

M. L. Samuels, *Linguistic Evolution, with Special Reference to English*.

Questions to Consider:

1. What are some of the reasons commonly given for the occurrence of the GVS?

2. How did the GVS contribute to the gap between writing and speech?

Lecture Fourteen—Transcript
The Great Vowel Shift and Modern English

If anybody has heard anything about the history of the English Language, it's probably the Great Vowel Shift. What was the Great Vowel Shift? Why does it matter, and why has it become a touchstone for the study of the history of the English language?

In spite of its portentous name, the Great Vowel Shift is really something very simple, but it had a huge impact on the sound and the shape of the English language between the time of Chaucer and the time of Shakespeare. Indeed, it is because of the Great Vowel Shift that the language of Chaucer was largely opaque by the time of Shakespeare. It is because no change in pronunciation as systematic or as radical as the Great Vowel Shift has happened since Shakespeare's time that Shakespeare's language is still relatively accessible to us.

During the period of the Great Vowel Shift—roughly from the middle of the 15th century to the end of the 16th and beginning of the 17th centuries—many other changes were going on in English. The vocabulary was increasing; syntax was changing; words were getting new meanings; and attitudes towards language use, regional variation and public idiom were changing dramatically. All of these things go on together with pronunciation to change irrevocably Middle English into what we might call early Modern English.

In subsequent lectures, I will be detailing these other changes, but for now I'd like to work through the Great Vowel Shift, and in this lecture, I'd like to work through the details of the sound changes. I'd also like to call attention to some ways in which scholars are able to use written documents to provide evidence for those changes in sound. And finally, I'd like to suggest some ways in which the Great Vowel Shift, if you like, has become not just a fact, but something of a myth of English linguistic history.

It may not be too much to say that the Great Vowel Shift is the single most important change that separates Middle English from Modern English. And it is also the change that separates English from the other European languages. Only six vowels were affected by the Great Vowel Shift and they were what we will call the long, stressed monophthongs—that is, they were vowels that were in stressed positions in the word; they were the vowels on which word emphasis fell. They were held for a long period of time. That means that there was a quantitative difference between these vowels and other vowels, and they were monophthongs—that is, they were single or pure sounds.

A monophthong is a single sound made by keeping the mouth in the same position:

/ɛ/   "eh" (*e* in *bet*)

/i/   "ee"

/o/   "oh"

/u/   "oo"

/ɔ/   "ah" (*o* in *mop*)

Are all monophthongs, because as you say them, your mouth stays in the same position; /ai/ is a diphthong—that is, it is a sound made up of two sounds. You can feel in saying a sound /ai/ or the sound /au/—as in *mice* and *house*—you can feel your mouth move from one position to the other. That is a diphthong.

The Great Vowel Shift affected the long, stressed monophthongs of Middle English, and they were /a/ with the letter "a" (the letter "a" represented the "ah" sound, as in the word *name*, pronounced "nahmeh"); the sound "eh," which was written with an "e," and that would have been in a word like F-E-E-T, pronounced "fate"; the sound /i/, which was written with an "i," and that would have been in a word like B-I-T-E ("beet"); the sound /o/, as in the word "do," which would have been written D-O (pronounced "dough"); and the sound /u/, which would have been written with a "u," and this would have been in a word like *mus* or *hus* ("moos" or "hoos"), *mouse* or *house*: A, E, I, O, and U.

These are still, by and large, the long vowels of the European languages. The Great Vowel Shift is responsible for the reason why we say A, E, I, O, U and not "ah," "eh," "ih," "oh," and "oo." So once you've got that, you're halfway there.

Don't be intimidated by the Great Vowel Shift. I'm going to try to explain how it happened and I'm going to have to go back to some of the material from one of my first lectures on articulatory phonetics.

You will remember that articulatory phonetics was the way in which we describe how vowels and consonants are produced in the mouth. When we describe vowels, we describe them according to their height in the mouth and according to their front or back position in the mouth.

Vowels can be low, middle, and high, and they can be back, mid and front. So if you think of it as a grid, you can place the vowels in that way. One point I want to make too before I get into the details of the Great Vowel Shift is something about long vowels. We very casually use a phrase like a "long vowel" or a "short vowel" today when we are signaling a qualitative difference in vowel sound—that is, the difference between "beet" and "bit." I think most people would say that "beet" has a long vowel and "bit" has a short vowel.

But this is not the way in which I and linguists use the terms "long" and "short." "Long" and "short" has to do with the qualitative difference—that is, the period of time through which you hold a vowel. In Old English and in Middle English, vowel length—that is, quantitative vowel length—was a meaningful difference in the language. What do I mean by this?

Let me give you an example. In Old English, you had two words that were spelled the same way: G-O-D. One of them was pronounced "gode," the other was pronounced "gooade." The first one meant *God*, and the second one meant *good*. The only difference between these words was the period of time you held that vowel: "gode," "gooade." Vowel length was, to be technical about it, a phonemic distinction. That means that depending on how long you held the vowel, you would signal a different meaning for that word.

Modern English has lost this distinction, and this distinction is lost during the period of the Great Vowel Shift. So let me give you an example. If I were to say, "sat"—S-A-T—and I were to say, "saat"—S-A-T—and the difference was only the period of time that I held the vowel, there would be no difference in meaning. You might think that I was being affected, or that I was stressing things, or that I had particular difficulty in speaking, but vowel length does not determine change in meaning.

In my teaching, I very often use this as an example, many years ago, a student raised her hand and said, "What about the difference between something that's 'bad' and something that's 'baad'?" Here, you have vowel length that may be uniquely phonemic in English. "Bad," held for a short period of time, means something that is bad. "Baad," held for a long period of time, means something that is good. So here may be one unique case in modern spoken English when quantitative vowel length makes a difference.

Now let's go to the details of the Great Vowel Shift. The Great Vowel Shift can be summarized as follows: the front vowels were raised and fronted, the back vowels were raised and retracted, and the high vowels were made into diphthongs. Let me clarify what all of that means. Here's one way in which we can think about the Great Vowel Shift—a scholarly reconstruction, if you like, of what happened.

You had two high front vowels in Middle English: You had the sound /i/ ["ee"] as in "me," M-Y or M-I ("mee-self") or "bee" (B-I or B-Y), or in a sound like "meese" (mice), M-I-C-E. That /i/ sound "ee," written /i/ in Middle English, is a high front vowel. It's pronounced high in the mouth and it's pronounced towards the front of the mouth: "ee."

The other high vowel is /u/ ["oo"], and you can feel that it is also high in the mouth: "oo." In Middle English, this was the sound in "hoose" (house), "moose" (mouse). What happened was /i/ and /u/ became diphthongs in the course of the Great Vowel Shift. That means that /i/ became /ai/ ["I"] and /u/ became /au/ ["ow"]. So "meese" became "mice" and "hoose" became "house."

By the end of the 16th century, these sounds would have probably been pronounced "moice" and "hause," and by the 17th century, they would have been pronounced "mice" and "house." This took a long period of time and in a few minutes, I'm going to talk about what happened in the course of this particular change.

Item number one: the high front vowels /i/ and /u/ become diphthongs /ai/ and /au/ over a long period of time. Second, you have mid vowels—that is, you have vowels that are pronounced in the middle of the mouth, and these are /e/ ["eh"] and /o/ ["oh"]. So Middle English *feet* (F-E-E-T), would be pronounced "fate." It came to be raised and fronted. "*Feet*" became "feet." *Do* (D-O), pronounced "dough", came to be pronounced as Modern English *do* ["doo"].

Then you had the low back vowels. In Middle English, the vowel indicated by the letter "a" would have been /a/ ["ah"]. So a word like "nahmeh" became "name." Now it's a full diphthong—"name"—but the important part is /a/ ["ah"], /e/ ["eh"]: "nahmeh," "name."

Finally, the long open /ɔ/ ["aw"] as in *so* ["saw,"] (S-O), came to be pronounced "so" in that way.

This is the way in which the Great Vowel Shift is believed to have worked. More than one explanation exists for it. Some scholars believe that during the 15th and 16th centuries, English dialects were in contact in new ways. Migrations from the north and the midlands into London brought speakers into contact. And this mix of dialects created social pressures to develop or to select a set of pronunciations that would have new social prestige.

The sounds that were chosen or that developed appear in retrospect to be the sounds of the Great Vowel Shift. Let me stress, this is not a case of people sitting down and saying, "We need to systematically change the way in which we speak, and what we're going to do is we're going to select a new set of sounds." What happened was there were many ways of pronouncing vowels—some of them regional, some of them historical—and over time, a particular system of pronunciation sorts itself out as an accepted standard form.

As a corollary to this contact of dialects and changes in pronunciation, what you also have is the loss of French. All cultures need a prestige form of language. Some cultures have a different language. In the Middle Ages in England, it was French. In Russia in the 19th century, it was French. In Rome during the 1st and 2nd centuries A.D., it was Greek—that is, you have a prestige language that signals class and education.

As French disappeared in the 15th century, if you like, a slot was opened for a prestige language. And what filled that slot was not a different language, but a different form of the English language. So what we see emerging in the course of the 15th and 16th centuries is a systematic change in pronunciation that in retrospect becomes the prestige or standard form of pronunciation and this is something that operates in tandem with the loss of French.

I want to go back for just a minute to those diphthongs. I mentioned that /ai/ and /au/ from /i/ and /u/ didn't become full diphthongs

©2008 The Teaching Company.

overnight. In the course of the 15th and part of the 16th centuries, you would say a word like *my*, not as Middle English "me," but more as something like "moy." You would say a word like *house* as something like "haoose"—that is, you would have a lower sound as your first sound in your diphthong.

So words like Modern English *bite* would be *boyte*, or words like Modern English *I* would be *oy*, and words like Modern English *fight* would be *foyt*. This, I believe, is the origin of "pirate English." We think of pirate English as that "aargh" sound matey—that late-17th-century Johnny Depp-ism of life. I want to suggest that what we think of as pirate English is in fact a regional evocation of early-17th-century English where the Great Vowel Shift has not fully run its course, and where the long, high, front monophthongs of Middle English have not fully diphthongized into their modern form: "Oy, matey!"

This form of pirate English, if anybody asks you, "How did the pirates speak?" you'd say, "They were in fact speaking a form of English in which the Great Vowel Shift hadn't fully realized its course, and in which the high, front monophthongs of Middle English hadn't fully diphthongized."

It's also true that the Great Vowel Shift hadn't fully run its course as late as the early 18th century in some areas of England. Alexander Pope, writing in the 18th century, reveals in his writings that the Great Vowel Shift hasn't run its course completely because he will rhyme a word like *join* (J-O-I-N) with a word like *line* (L-I-N-E), and they were probably pronounced "joyn" "loyn," and they rhymed.

I'm told that there are pockets in America where regional speakers will say things like, "We're going to draw the 'loyn' somewhere and we're going to 'joyn' up." It's still that early sound in forms of regional English. Pope can do that rhyme on *line* and *join* because the diphthongs haven't fully mutated, if you like, into their modern form.

We can use rhyme, as I'm suggesting, as evidence for the Great Vowel Shift, but we can also use writing, and in particular the writing of personal letters. During the 15th and the 16th centuries there was a rise in the writing of personal letters among some of the great families of England—gentry families, commercial families—as the children were leaving the family stead to go to London or to the city. The families wrote letters to each other. Many of these letters still survive.

What we have in many of these letters from families known as the Pastons and the Sellies and the Stoners—the *Paston Letters* in particular remain one of the richest troves of personal epistolarity for English literary history—what we have here are educated, somewhat educated people. Let me be more precise—people of varying degrees of education, some of whom learned to write in Chancery schools and used Chancery forms, some of whom used older Middle English spellings, some of whom were reflecting their actual speech habits.

What you can see in a set of letters from roughly the middle of the 15th to the beginning of the 16th century are attempts on the part of these writers to represent the changing sounds of English. Let me give you some examples.

Very often you will see the word *meet* (M-E-E-T)—to meet together—spelled M-Y-T-E. This is Old English, but it's used in a different way—that is, what they're saying is, "We're going to meet." In Middle English, M-E-E-T would have been pronounced "mayt"—"We're going to mayt together." If you wanted to say, "We're going to meet together," you would have to write, M-I- or M-Y-T-E. They're using an old Middle English convention of spelling to indicate a new sound.

Similarly, the verb *to hear*—to hear something—H-E-A-R, ["hare"] in Middle English, is now being spelled with a "y" or an "I": *hyre*. So they're using old conventions of spelling to indicate new sounds. When we see these spellings, what we say is, "Here are people who are trying to write to reflect a change in pronunciation."

In Middle English, if you wanted to stay somewhere, you would "abeed," A-B-I-D-E. We say "abide" because the /i/ has become a diphthong. In the 15th and 16th centuries, when these families are writing to each other, they will sometimes spell it, A-B-E-Y-D, *abeyed*, because they want to show that that /i/ sound has become a diphthong. So here you have a new spelling that's designed to evoke a new sound. Our, O-U-R, in Middle English, this would have been pronounced, *aur, aurselven, ourselves*.

In many of these letters, it is spelled A-U-R, to indicate that it is not "uurr" but "our." *Out*—I'm going *out*—would have been pronounced in Middle English I'm going *owt*. This is being spelled O-W-T. In other words, it's an imagined or created spelling to indicate that the diphthong has happened.

I have found in some of these letters the word *house*, which in Middle English would have been spelled H-U-S, and pronounced *hoos*, I have seen it written H-O-W-S, *hows*, because the scribes and the writers are telling us, "This is how we said it."

These are examples—there are many, many others—but these are examples of how you can see individuals in England trying to evoke the sound of language changing. They use either old spelling conventions or they make up new or ad-hoc spellings in order to do that.

So, what I would like to do in concluding is review some of the material here with the previous lecture and look ahead to the next, to try to understand why the Great Vowel Shift is important, but why it needs to be understood as part of a larger set of changes that are moving Middle English to Modern English.

First: the growing gap between educated writing and speech. You'll remember that what Chancery had done was it had set up a system of spelling that was designed for official documents, and that could be learned by a scribe regardless from what regional area that scribe had come from. That spelling is gradually becoming conventionalized and becoming divorced from speech. Spelling no longer, in effect, represents pronunciation.

Caxton, by setting up his press at Westminster and by printing the works of English literature in Chancery spelling forms, is using an official standard as a literary standard and he's also, in effect, historically, therefore, decoupling the earlier language from its spelling forms. In other words, you're reading a somewhat modernized Chaucer.

What's going on here is also a change in punctuation. One of the fascinating features of the history of the English language is precisely the way in which punctuation changes. One could indeed give an entire set of lectures on the history of punctuation. Let me just give you a little bit now.

During the Middle Ages and during the period largely of manuscript transmission, punctuation is eye punctuation—in other words, punctuation is designed to move the eye. [Earlier,] punctuation is ear punctuation. It is designed to mirror the sound rather than the sense—that is, what punctuation is designed to do is indicate how something should be read aloud. The job of punctuation in the manuscript age is the job not of marking clauses, but of marking breath.

Let me reiterate, that early punctuation is ear punctuation. It signals breaks in reading aloud. By Caxton's time, punctuation is moving toward eye punctuation—that is, it's designed for the silent reader, signaling syntactic or clausal units of a sentence. Commas, semicolons, periods and the like are designed to break up sentences into units of meaning, rather than into units of breath. This is something that is also affecting the look of English.

What we see in the history of the 15th and the 16th centuries is a systematic change in the pronunciation of the long, stressed monophthongs—a gradual divorce between spelling conventions and speech—but at the same time, an attempt on the part of some individual writers to try to get their spelling to mime or to reproduce changing sounds.

As a coda to this lecture, let me mention a small group of words that seem not to have undergone the Great Vowel Shift. There are a small group of words spelled with an "ea": *steak*, *great*, *break*, and *yea*. If these had participated in the Great Vowel Shift, they would have been *steek*, *greet*, *breek*, and *yee*. This is not something that affects every single word with an "ea," it is not something which affects lots and lots of names that are spelled with "ea," but etymologically and historically, the words *steak*, *great*, *break*, and *yea* should have participated in the Great Vowel Shift and been pronounced "steek," "greet," "breek," and "yee."

Why this is, nobody knows. So I'm going to leave you with this provocation—that even though linguists may think they can explain everything, there are gaps in our knowledge and exceptions to our rules. In subsequent lectures, I'm going to be opening up many of these gaps and fissures in our knowledge to show us how the writers and the readers of the 16th, 17th and 18th centuries sought, but sought in vain to fix, to regulate and to manipulate a language that was changing far too fast for anyone to transcribe.

Lecture Fifteen
The Expanding English Vocabulary

Scope:

In the years 1500 through 1700, the vocabulary of English grew dramatically. New words were borrowed from the disciplines of experimental science, classical scholarship, and practical technology. New words were coined from Latin and Greek to express technical concepts and to enrich or beautify the English language. Imperial exploration also brought with it a host of words from new worlds.

This lecture shows how to organize this increase in lexical material according to disciplines of entry into the language. It also illustrates how words, both new and old, were changing in meaning, and how the phenomenon of polysemy (the multiple meanings or connotations of words) affected English writing.

Outline

I.   During the period of the GVS, the English language vocabulary was also changing dramatically, with words coming in from science, colonial exploration, and philosophy, and from all languages of the world. In this lecture, we'll look at the raw increase in words in the English vocabulary, as well as how English came to be omnivorous in its verbiage.

   A. In the mid-15th century, we see what are known as "inkhorn terms" coming into the language. These are words coined from Latin or Greek for "educated" effect and sonic power.

   1.   Such words were perceived to come right from the inkhorn, or inkwell, and thus were a mark of reading and writing rather than of speech.

   2.   Although inkhorn terms also identified the user as educated, they were sometimes the object of derision by those who felt they had little rational basis in the history of the language.

   3.   Some examples of inkhorn terms still in the language include *allurement, anachronism, autograph, capsule, dexterous, disregard* (first used by Milton), *erupt,* and *meditate.*

B. In poetry, the corresponding concept for inkhorn terms is "aureate diction," a term that depicts new or unusual coinages as "glistening" or "golden" in their Latinity.

    1. As we've seen thus far, Chaucer, Caxton, and other writers saw English as a mutable language; John of Trevisa went so far as to say that the English language had been *apeyred*, that is, watered down or corrupted.

    2. Many early writers held the parallel view that Latin or the Romance languages were somehow immutable and, thus, of a higher level than English. For this reason, poets used an aureate diction that was highly polysyllabic and often relied on metaphors of beauty, visual splendor, sweetness, and purification.

C. In the *Art of Rhetoric* (1553), Thomas Wilson uses terms from aureate and inkhorn diction to mock the affectation of writers of his day. His parody of a letter of application from a subordinate to a superior sounds like double-talk.

D. Some inkhorn terms did not remain in the language, including *adepted* (*attained*), *adnichilate* (*reduced to nothing*), *obstupefact* (*to make unclear*), and *temulent* (*drunk*).

II. Words also entered the language from travel, commercial contact, and science.

A. Commerce and contact with European countries brought new words into English. Examples include the following:

    1. France: *alloy, bigot, bombast, duel, entrance, equip, essay, explore, mustache, progress, talisman, tomato, volunteer.*

    2. Italy: *argosy* (itself an Italian coinage based on the Greek epic *The Odyssey*), *balcony, granite, stanza, violin, volcano.*

    3. Spain and Portugal: *anchovy, armada, banana, cannibal, cocoa, embargo, maize, mulatto, potato, tobacco, yam.*

    4. Dutch: *smuggler, cruise, jib, schooner, reef, walrus, blunderbuss, tattoo, knapsack.*

B. Notice how many of these words reflect colonial contact, especially in the Americas and Africa. These are not just words from different languages, but words that enter into the register of colonization and military engagement.

C. Words from non-European languages entered through travel, trade, and conquest. Examples include the following:

    1. Arabic: *sash, hashish, mohair, sherbet, sofa, henna.*

    2. Turkish: *dolman, coffee, caftan, kiosk.*

    3. Chinese: *ketchup.*

    4. African: *zebra.*

    5. North American languages: *raccoon, moose, skunk, hickory, totem, canoe.*

D. Words also arrived from science and other intellectual pursuits, including:

    1. Natural sciences: *vertebra, torpor, specimen, spectrum, mica, lens.*

    2. Mathematics: *chord, cylinder, prism, calculus.*

    3. Philosophy: *dogma, critic, curriculum, crux, propaganda, alibi.*

III. The growth of the English vocabulary prompted several discussions about whether loan words or new coinages of these kinds were in keeping with what was called the "genius" of the English language.

A. In the 16th–18th centuries, many writers were concerned with the question of whether these new words were diluting the language.

B. English was known to be a Germanic language, and some scholars believed that the perceived encroachments from overly-learned Latin or from the affected (even effeminate) French were changing the overarching structure of the language.

C. Such questions were also part of a larger turn in education toward an understanding of the "excellence" of English; in other words, the study of language became a way of reinforcing cultural politics by other means.

    1. English schoolmasters of the 16th and 17th centuries frequently reflected on the nature of English.

    2. Alexander Gil (1564–1635), headmaster of St. Paul's School and Milton's teacher, was interested in pronunciation and developed a system of phonetic transcription with an eye toward spelling reform. He also advocated the exclusion of new words and inkhorn terms from the language.

3. In his *Logonomia Anglica* (*The English Language*) of 1619, Gil rails against Chaucer as a corrupter of language. According to Gil, "feral monsters of words" are being brought into English daily, so that the language is no longer a peaceable kingdom of Eden but a horrific zoo of the linguistic imagination.

4. Note the degree to which Gil's language seems Miltonic. Gil writes of "horrid, evil-sounding magpies," while Milton speaks of Satan's "horrid crew" and the "horrid silence of the fallen." For Gil, English now represents a bastard tongue, and in Book II of *Paradise Lost*, Satan discovers his own bastard progeny, sin.

5. The paradise that has been lost for Gil is a paradise of language, while Milton sees the loss of ethics and morality.

IV. The changing vocabulary of English was affected not simply by this new world of words but also by a phenomenon known as "polysemy": As new words entered the language and as science and technology began to inform the discourses of poetry and prose, words began to change meaning and connotation.

A. During the 16th century, the rise in commercial vocabulary offered literary writers new possibilities for metaphorical relationships; in other words, social relationships and personal desire came to be expressed in commercial terms. We will see this later, especially in Shakespeare.

1. As you may recall, the word *cheap* (meaning *exchange*, a place of commerce) originated as a borrowing from Latin into the Germanic languages during the continental period. But during the 15th–17th centuries, writers also discovered that the word could be used for punning or wordplay.

2. The same is true of such words as *flagrant* or *ardent* (originally meaning *on fire*), which gradually acquired emotional meanings associated with love.

3. Polysemy made possible greater ambiguities in vocabulary and a wider range of figurative or metaphorical diction in poetry and prose.

B. We will see in the subsequent study of dictionaries how the problem of the literal versus the metaphorical use of a word comes to dominate the organization of word definitions, and how our dictionaries reflect not so much a record of actual speech as a system of definitional organization worked out by 17th- and 18th-century schoolmasters.

Reading:

Albert C. Baugh and Thomas M. Cable, *A History of the English Language*.

E. J. Dobson, *English Pronunciation, 1500–1700*.

Terttu Nevalainen, "Early Modern English Lexis and Semantics," in Roger Lass, ed., *The Cambridge History of the English Language*, Vol. 3: 1476–1776.

M. L. Samuels, *Linguistic Evolution, with Special Reference to English*.

Questions to Consider:

1. What are "inkhorn terms," and are they still popular today?

2. What is polysemy, and how did it enrich—or merely confuse—the vocabulary of English?

Lecture Fifteen—Transcript
The Expanding English Vocabulary

In the middle of the 17th century, a dictionary of the English language was published with the title *A New World of Words*. My subject in this lecture is that new world of words, and I mean that in several ways. Certainly during the period that the Great Vowel Shift was going on, the English language's vocabulary was also changing dramatically. New words were coming in from science, from colonial exploration and exploitation, from ways of understanding, and from structures of experience; from all forms of new coinages and all languages of the world—European and non-European.

The *New World of Words* evokes the sense that English drew its vocabulary from the globe, and just as the search for a new world brought economic riches to the old, so it brought linguistic riches to the old.

In this lecture, I want to look at the rise of the English vocabulary, not just the raw increase in words, but the way in which English became what it is today—a language omnivorous, voracious in its verbiage.

When we think of the expanding English vocabulary, we need to think of it in several levels, or several strata. The earliest set of terms to come in, in the period I'm discussing now—the mid-15th century—were terms that were called "inkhorn" terms. That is, words coined from Latin or Greek, and they were coined for "educated" effect, or for sonic power. They were called inkhorn terms because they seemed to come right out of the inkwell, or right out of the inkhorn. In other words, they were a mark, not of speech, but of reading and writing.

Even though they were a mark of education by the user, they could be the object of derision by those who felt that they had little rational basis in the history of the language. What are some of these inkhorn terms from this period of time that are still in the English language? Here are a few of them in alphabetical order: *allurement*; *anachronism*; *autograph*; *capsule*; *dexterous*; *disregard* (that, by the way, is not an early inkhorn but a late inkhorn term that's first used by John Milton); *erupt*; and *meditate*.

What you can hear in the inkhorn words is that they are polysyllabic, that they are words of Latin or Greek origin, and that they are built up of roots with prefixes and suffixes. Inkhorn terms fill the learned prose of the early Modern period. In poetry, the corresponding term for inkhorn is "aureate"—aureate diction.

Aureate means *golden*. New coinages and new loans were brought in, and this was called "aureation," because the words appeared glistening or golden in their Latinity. There was the belief, as we've seen throughout the course, that English was a mutable language. We live, as Caxton said, under the domination of the moon—things are transitory. As Chaucer put it in *Troilus and Criseyde*, "Meanings change and regional variation makes it hard for us to understand what someone in a different part of the country may be saying."

In John of Trevisa's words, "The birth tongue of English has been *apeyred* …" That is, watered down, diluted, corrupted in the way that one would alloy base metal with gold.

This view of the native root stock of English contributed to a parallel view that Latin or the Romance languages were somehow immutable—in other words, that if English was a language of brass, Latin was a language of gold. So the poets used an aureate diction that was highly polysyllabic, that relied on metaphors of beauty, of visual splendor, of sweetness, of purification. These were the aureate terms. You can see aureation and inkhornism coming together in one of the most important educational treatises written in the middle of the 16th century.

Thomas Wilson's *Art of Rhetoric* was first written in 1553. He uses terms from aureate and inkhorn diction to parody or mock the level of affectation that writers of his day had used. I'm going to give you just a couple of sentences from this passage. Wilson is writing, in effect, a parody of a letter of application—that is, a letter written by a subordinate to a superior where the subordinate is asking for the superior's help or benefit, and where the subordinate is making himself seem even less than the superior.

I'm just going to read these two sentences and I'm going to read them in Modern English pronunciation, but I want you to hear them because I want you to see how many of these words you really understand. The writer writes:

Ponderyng expendyng, and reuolutyng with my self your ingent affabilite, and ingenious capacitee, for mundane affaires; I cannot but celebrate and extolle your magnificall dexteritee, aboue all other.

What is this writer saying? The writer is saying that:

As I think about what a smart and wonderful person you are, and how great you are in the life in this world, I can do nothing but praise it.

That's what he's saying, but *pondering, expending, revoluting, indigent affability, ingenious capacity, mundane affairs*. (We think of *mundane* as being not worthy of discussion, but *mundane* comes from *mundis*, meaning the earth. So mundane affairs really are not low, but high—worldly affairs.) *Celebrate, extol, your magnificall dexterity*—that is, your ability to do these things—your dexterity. *Dexterity* comes from the Latin *dexter*, meaning the *right hand*. The opposite of the right hand was *sinister*—that is, the *left hand*. So if you were dexterous, you were right-handed, and if you were sinister, you were left-handed. Not just your magnificent, but your *magnificall* dexterity.

I'm spending time with these sentences to show you how the vocabulary of the English language in the 16th century was expanding by using these coinages that came out of learning. Some of these terms survive today, but there are some inkhorn terms that do not. I would like to share with you some of my favorites, or, to put it more pointedly, I'd like to advocate the return of *adepted*, which meant *attained*; *adnichilate*, which means *to reduce to nothing—ad-nichil-ate—to bring to nothing*; *obstupefact, to make unclear*; and one of my favorites, *temulent*, meaning *drunk*. It seems to me that we have so many words for inebriation that one more certainly couldn't hurt, and I would like to vote for *temulent*.

Why words stayed and why some disappeared nobody really knows. But words entered English during this period not only from the inkhorn, but from the ship. They entered the language from travel, from commercial contact, and from science. What I'm going to be doing for the most part in the remainder of this lecture is giving you lists of words—in other words, words that have come from other languages during this period of time.

©2008 The Teaching Company.

From France, during the period of exploration, contact, war, and social expansion, we have the following, just as a small sample: *alloy, bigot, bombast, duel, entrance, equip, essay, explore, mustache, progress, talisman, tomato, volunteer*. What do these words have in common other than that they come from French? Well, they certainly have an evocation of style, of the exotic, of forms of behavior, and also of things brought from the New World, like the tomato.

Words at this time that come from Italy are very often words for Italian things: *argosy*—that is, a great journey. Now this is an Italian learned coinage that's based on a Greek myth, because you had *The Odyssey* which was the journey of Odysseus. The Argosy was the journey of the Argo, which was the name of Jason's ship in the myth of the story of *The Golden Fleece*. So the Italian scholars coined *argosy* and it was brought into England. *Balcony*—how can one not imagine Romeo and Juliette in Verona without that balcony? That is a word from Italian. *Granite*—the great quarries were Italian, and so granite comes from Italy. *Stanza*—the Italians developed the stanza as the medium of lyric and narrative poetry. *Violin*—Cremona and the Stradivarius and the Amati families making violins. If you think of one thing Italian, you think of the *volcano*, whether it be Etna or Pompeii.

From Spain and from Portugal words entered English not simply from those languages, but also from the way in which the Spanish and the Portuguese named things from non-European contexts. What are we talking about here? We're talking about new fish, new fruits, new vegetables, new things like *anchovy, armada*—the Spanish Armada—*banana, cannibal, cocoa, embargo, maize* (meaning *corn*), *mulatto, potato, tobacco*, and *yam*.

Many words came from Dutch and these also were words that were grounded in maritime exploration: *smuggler, cruise, jib, schooner, reef, walrus, blunderbuss, tattoo*, and *knapsack*. Notice how many of these words reflect colonial contact, especially in the Americas and in Africa. These are not just words from different languages, but they are words from different registers. They enter into the registers of colonialization and military engagement. Words from non-European languages entered through travel, through trade, and through conquest.

So as English and Europeans came in contact with speakers of Arabic—not just in the Middle East but along the great slave routes of the Indian Ocean and soon the Atlantic—they found words like *sash, hashish, mohair, sherbet, sofa,* and *henna*. From Turkish: *dolman, coffee, caftan, kiosk*. In Chinese, the word for a flavored fish sauce eventually came to be pronounced as *ketchup*. In Africa, there was the *zebra*, and in North America, there was the *raccoon*, the *moose*, the *skunk*, the *hickory*, the *totem*, and the *canoe*.

It was a new world of words all right, but it was also a new world, not just from colonialism, but from science of expansion. From the natural sciences, and from the study of the human body and the animal form, new words were being coined such as: *vertebra, torpor, specimen, spectrum, mica, lens*. In mathematics: *chord, cylinder, prism, calculus*. From philosophy: *dogma, critic, curriculum, crux, propaganda,* and *alibi*.

The growth of the English vocabulary prompted several discussions about whether loan words or new coinages of these kind were in keeping with what was called the genius of the English language. I can reel off, as I have, lists and lists of words, but the question really is not just whether these individual words are, should be, or became English, the question that was asked at this time—the 16th, the 17th, and the 18th centuries—the question that was asked was really, are these new words *apeyring*—breaking down, diluting, changing the wellsprings of language?

We've seen to this point in the course that English historically is a member of the Germanic languages branch. Was English a Germanic language at this time? Some scholars felt that the encroachments from overly-learned Latin, or what was believed to be affected—indeed, even effeminate—French, were changing the overarching structure of the language. Such questions were also at the heart of a turn toward education in what came to be called the "excellence" of English.

The study of language during the 16th and the 17th centuries, as I will develop in this and in my subsequent lectures, was really a study of, if you like, cultural politics—doing spelling, doing vocabulary, was doing nationalism.

There were many English schoolmasters of the 16th and 17th centuries who reflected on these problems and their writings fill volumes in great libraries. In this and in the next few lectures, I'm going to be drawing on many of their writings for insights into what people at the time thought the English language was doing.

The figure on whom I wish to concentrate now was a man named Alexander Gil, who lived from 1564 to 1635. He was the headmaster of the great St. Paul's School and he was the teacher of John Milton. Gil is, to me, a fascinating figure in the history of the English language. He's very interested in pronunciation, and among the many things he does is to develop a system, if you like, of phonetic transcription—that is, he tries to come up with a way of actually spelling to reflect a form of pronunciation—but his idea of pronunciation is a highly-educated and rarified one.

Gil is also fascinating because he writes vehemently against the introduction of these inkhorn terms, these aureate words, these new Latin and Romance forms. Gil is a genius at exaggeration, and in 1619, he published a book called *The Logonomia Anglica*—that is on *The English Language*. He's writing in Latin. I'm going to quote him in an English translation, but I'm going to also pay a little bit of attention to his Latin.

Gil is very much against what we might call the lexical enhancements and the rhetorical amplifications of his time. Just the century before, I'd illustrated how Thomas Wilson could parody aureate and inkhorn language in courtly prose. Gil is looking back to a time further in the past. He's interested in what he calls "the language of our forefathers in antiquity," and he believes that no language other than English could be, in his words, I'm translating now, "graceful, elegant or apt for the expression of every subtle thought, but faults," he says, "have crept in." He announces with a vehemence worthy of Milton, his most famous student, the following. And now I'm going to read an extended paragraph from Gil in a Modern English translation of his Latin. He writes:

> About the year 1400, Geoffrey Chaucer, star of ill-omen, rendered his poetry notorious by the use of Latin and French words. Such is the stupidity of the uneducated masses that they admire most what they least comprehend: from that time on a new scurry appeared in writing and speaking, for since everyone wishes to appear as a smatterer of tongues and to vaunt his proficiency in Latin, French (or any other

language), so daily wild beasts of words are tamed, and horrid evil-sounding magpies and owls of unpropitious birth are taught to hazard our words. Thus today we are, for the most part, Englishmen not speaking English and not understood by English ears. Nor are we satisfied with having begotten this illegitimate progeny, nourished this monster, but we have exiled that which was legitimate—our birthright—pleasant in expression, and acknowledged by our forefathers. O cruel country!

This is one of the most brilliantly insane passages in the history of the English language, but its brilliance and its insanity can be parsed. What I want to stress here is that Gil sees Chaucer, not as the enhancer of language, which is what many saw him as, but as the corrupter of language—that is, that Gil is also concerned with the way in which this influx of Latin and romance terms has changed the way in which we speak and has challenged English. Also he creates a set of metaphors that we need to get behind this English and look at his Latin to understand.

When he says, "Wild beasts of words are tamed," what he's saying in Latin is *"ita quotidie [thus every day] fera vocum monstra cicuriat"—the feral monsters of words are tamed.* It's as if words are beasts and these beasts are being brought into a language that has now become not a peaceable kingdom of Eden, but a horrific zoo of the linguistic imagination. These are horrid evil-sounding magpies. His word *horrid* is the word *horridus* in Latin. The Latin word *horrid* means to *bristle*, it means *bristling*, and this is a word that will become central to the vocabulary of Gil's most famous student, John Milton.

Gil represents an English now as a bastard tongue; a monster living in the house that should be the home of the legitimate. And I just want to pause here and just call to your attention how Miltonic his language is. I cannot but imagine John Milton, decades later, blind, composing *Paradise Lost*, thinking of his teacher. Horrid—right from *Paradise Lost's* start, we hear of Satan's horrid crew; Hell is a horrible dungeon; there's the horrid silence of the fallen; Moloch is a horrid king.

And in Book II of *Paradise Lost*, Satan discovers his own illegitimate and bastard progeny.

... pensive, here I sat [says Sin, daughter of Satan]
Alone ... till my womb,
Pregnant by thee, and now excessive grown
Prodigious motion felt and rueful throes.
At this last odious offspring whom thou seest
Thine own begotten, breaking violent way,
Tore through my entrails ..."

This is Sin talking to Satan about how Satan is the father in this incestuous coupling. The daughter of Satan speaking to the father, the horrors of the illegitimate are everywhere in Milton.

I'm suggesting that Gil's vocabulary affects Milton's mind, and that what Milton is doing is he's looking back to Gil's view of a fall from a linguistic Eden. The paradise that has been lost for Gil is a paradise of language. The paradise that Milton sees is a paradise of ethics, morality, and of experience. I want these things to be held in your mind as we work through in subsequent lectures— the relationship between the poetry and prose of the time.

In wrapping up, the changing vocabulary of English was affected not simply by this new world of words, but by a phenomenon known as "polysemy." As these new words entered the language, and as science and technology began to inform the discourses of poetry and prose, words began to change meaning and connotation. What happens in the 16th century is a rise in a commercial vocabulary that provides literary writers with new possibilities for metaphorical relationships. Social relationships and personal desire can be expressed in commercial terms. We're going to see this, in particular, when we look at the language of Shakespeare.

Let me just give you an example of some of these polysemous phenomena. The word *cheap*, for example, comes from Old English, and it also is a borrowing, you'll remember, from the continental period from Latin into the Germanic languages; it means *exchange* or a place of commerce—East Cheap is still a street in London. It's the eastern market. *Good cheap* was a *good value,* and things that were *valued cheaply* were *inexpensive.*

So you have *cheap,* meaning an experience of economics, of trade, of exchange, and then something very, very specific. But during the period of the 15th, 16th, and 17th centuries, the word connoted this range of meanings and it could be used polysemously—that is, it could be used for pun, it could be used for word play. Or words like *flagrant* or *ardent*, which originally mean *on fire* or *burning*, gradually come to take on emotional meanings—that is, someone who is *ardently* in love may be *burning* in love, but may not be on fire.

What polysemy does during this period is it makes possible greater ambiguities in vocabulary, and it makes possible a greater range of figurative or metaphorical diction in poetry and in prose. So what we see is how the changing vocabulary provokes an increase in the raw number of words and a set of changes in those words, bringing them into greater metaphorical, or greater figurative resonance.

What we will see in subsequent lectures is how schoolmasters, dictionary-makers, and poets are faced precisely with this problem of the literal's relationship to the metaphorical. One of the central problems in dictionary-making for the 17th and 18th centuries will precisely be how you distinguish between literal and figurative uses. So our dictionaries are reflecting not so much a record of actual speech, as a system of definitional organization worked out by the 17th- and 18th-century schoolmasters.

When we look at the writings of those schoolmasters, as I will in subsequent lectures, and when we look at the products of those schoolmasters—poets like Shakespeare and Milton—we're going to be looking at a collocation of writers using the English language and writers writing about the English language who are trying to locate themselves as firmly and precisely in the forests of this new world of words.

Lecture Sixteen
Early Modern English Syntax and Grammar

Scope:

In 1500, English syntax and grammar, while recognizable, still remained full of features that, to us, now seem odd and archaic. By 1700, the major patterns of word order and word endings, as well as the full modern system of pronouns, had crystallized into what we can see as virtually indistinguishable from our own. How did this happen?

This lecture traces the specifics of syntax and grammar in the period of Early Modern English to show how, in many ways, the shape of our modern language depends on some very small elements—in particular, the rise of the verbs *do* and *will* in new uses and the expansion of the forms of verbs and nouns ending in "-ing." We also look at changes in the system of modal (or helping) verbs and the second- and third-person pronouns. Even such a small problem as the difference between *its* and *it's* says a great deal about how English speakers make grammatical distinctions. We close the lecture with a reading of a scene from Shakespeare's play *Henry IV, Part I*, as a play about little words.

Outline

I. Our last lecture was essentially the story of "big words" in English: aureate and inkhorn vocabulary terms; new words from the worlds of science, technology, exploration, and colonization; and words from European and non-European languages. In this lecture, we'll deal with two little words, *do* and *will*, and a suffix, "-ing," that so radically changed their function and meaning in the 16th and 17th centuries that we might say the very shape of modern spoken idiomatic English hinges on their changes.

II. Although the GVS had changed pronunciation from Middle English, and the influx of words in the 16th and 17th centuries is still represented in our vocabulary today, the English of this period is not Modern English. That said, however, the highly idiomatic quality of Modern spoken English is a legacy from the time of Shakespeare.

A. The term "idiom" relates to expressions that are, in a sense, more than the sum of their constituent parts. For example, the dictionary meanings of *get*, *over*, *under*, *into*, and *out of* would not tell us the meaning of such expressions as *get over*, *get under*, *get into*, *get out of*, or *get up on*.

B. A large part of the idiomatic quality of English comes from developments in the 16th and 17th centuries, including changes in the verb *do*.

    1. As a full verb, *do* means to perform an action: "I did this." This usage appears in Old English; it is the oldest and most sustained use of the verb.

    2. *Do* can also be used as a replacement verb: "I went to the store, and having done that …" Here, the verb *do* replaces the verb *go* in the second part of the sentence; this usage developed in the Middle English period.

    3. In the Early Modern English period, *do* also came to be used as a periphrastic, or place-holding verb, in questions: "Do you know the way?" This represents a change from the earlier inversion of word order to ask a question: "Know you the way?"

    4. Finally, *do* emerged in the 16th century as an emphatic modal, or helping, verb: "I do know the answer."

III. In addition to these changing forms of *do*, we can also see changes in the forms of the suffix "-ing."

A. Old English had words that ended in "-ing" or "-ung" (as did all Germanic languages) to indicate, in nouns, ownership or genealogy, or to turn a verb into a noun. For example, *Hrunting* is the name of a sword; in *Beowulf*, the *Scyldings* are a clan or a family. Further, in Modern German (as in Old and Middle English), the "-ung" ending is used to signal a verb turned into a noun, or a concept noun.

B. In the Middle English period, "-ing" forms as participles (e.g., *going*, *having*, *doing*) were used only in Southern dialects. In Northern and Midland English dialects, participles were formed with "ende" or "ande" (e.g., *lovande*, *loving*).

C. In the 16th century, some of these dialectical forms entered into the metropolitan standard, as follows:

1. Expressions such as "The x being y, he did this" ("The house being on fire, he ran out").
2. Expressions such as "the x-ing of the y" ("the mowing of the grass," "the growing of the grain"), an idiom that did not appear until the late 16th century.
3. Expressions such as "don't blame me for having done it." Shakespeare was really the first writer to use this form.
4. New ways of expressing perfect tenses: "I have been waiting; I had been waiting." Note that these examples express the past in different ways. In the first, the action began in the past and continues into the present. In the second, the action began in the past, continued for some time, then ended in the past.
5. New ways of expressing the future: "I am going to get something to eat." Although this last form appeared by the late 16th century, it did not gain currency until the 19th.

D. Idiomatic Modern English is founded on changes such as these. They do not simply alter the way we speak, but they become characteristic of the way we speak.

IV. New forms of pronouns also took shape in the same period.

A. Sixteenth-century English inherited the remains of the older Middle English system of second-person pronouns.
1. The plural and formal forms were *you, ye,* and *your.*
2. The singular and informal forms were *thou, thee,* and *thine.*

B. The third-person pronoun, *it,* signals the neuter. As you recall, grammatical gender began to disappear in the Late Old English period, to be replaced by natural gender. In the 16th and 17th centuries, gender and grammatical relationships played themselves out in the words *it* and *its.*
1. Even as late as Shakespeare and the King James Bible, grammatical gender was still used, although perhaps as an archaism. In *The Merchant of Venice,* for example, Shakespeare writes, "How far that little candle throws his beams!"
2. We can see the possessive of *it* (*its*) sorting itself out in *King Lear*: "That nature which condemns it origin."

3. When we note such cracks and fissures in grammar, we're really seeing the language in flux.

V. We can also point to changes in the system of verbs during this period.

   A. Modal verbs, or helping verbs, include *shall, will, can, may,* and *ought.* These verbs can modify the tense or mood of a main verb but cannot by themselves be the only verb in a sentence. In Modern spoken English, they are not transitive verbs because they cannot take an object alone.

   B. Originally, these modals were full verbs. In the 17th century, for example, it would be grammatical to say, "I can music," meaning "I have a certain skill in music." In the 14th century, Chaucer wrote, "I shall to God and you," meaning "I am indebted to God and you."

   C. In the 16th and 17th centuries, these verbs changed usage and meaning.

      1. The distinctions between *shall/should, will/would, may/might,* and *can/could* arose during this period to create a subjunctive mood in English comparable to that in Latin. The subjunctive in Latin was used to express the counterfactual (something that hadn't happened) and the optative (desire): "O, that she would love me." This usage was deliberately designed in the 16th and 17th centuries to evoke a Latin grammatical category.

      2. *Shall/will* came to be restricted for forms of the future, losing their full verbal sense by the end of the 16th century. *Shall* was no longer used as a form of obligation, and *will* no longer expressed an individual's will or desire.

         a. In Bible translation, *will* was used to translate Latin *volo*, the verb meaning desire or volition; *shall* came to be used for a general future tense.

         b. In everyday speech, the distinction came to be one of emphasis. Schoolchildren were once taught that *I shall, you will, he will* were the standard, non-emphatic forms of expressing futurity; *I will, you shall, he shall* were considered emphatic.

   D. The central question that emerges here is: Are we talking about grammatical or stylistic changes? Where do we draw the line between grammar and idiom? Changes such as the ones we've seen in this lecture seem to have made Modern spoken English more idiomatic than it once was.

VI. A different kind of colloquialism seems to have emerged with these changes that has an important relationship to the language of ritual.

    A. Such phrases as "How's it going?" or "How do you do?" have become idioms of everyday speech, but they rely on grammatical forms newly developed in the 16th and 17th centuries.

    B. A scene from Shakespeare's play *Henry IV, Part I*, shows us the language of ritual evoked in a new way at a time when the changes in forms of *do* and *will* would have been palpable and pointed. Prince Hal replies to a plea from Falstaff not to be banished with "I do, I will," using *do* in the new sense of a replacement for Falstaff's verb, *banish*.

    C. In 1549, Archbishop Thomas Cranmer compiled the *Book of Common Prayer*, which served, over the next five decades, in various revisions, as the base text for English Protestantism. We're all familiar with the marriage ceremony in this book and its affirmation: "Wilt thou have this woman to thy wedded wife?" "I will."

        1. In the scene from Shakespeare's play and the ritual from the *Book of Common Prayer*, we see that *do* and *will* have become the new loci of English understanding and identity.

        2. In the comic scene of power in Shakespeare, Hal uses these words in profound ways. His pledges to Falstaff are not promises of unity but of divorce.

        3. As we'll see in subsequent lectures, Shakespeare and some of his contemporaries were masters of the new world of words, the expansion of vocabulary, and polysemy; Shakespeare, too, was a master of the little words *do* and *will*, whose changes radically affected the rituals of power and desire in early modern England.

Reading:

Matti Rissanen, "Syntax," in Roger Lass, ed., *The Cambridge History of the English Language*, Vol. 3: 1476–1776.

M. L. Samuels, *Linguistic Evolution, with Special Reference to English*.

Questions to Consider:

1. Give examples of how English grammar and syntax changed during the Early Modern English period.

2. Give other examples of how the language of contemporary ritual reflects the historical roots of English.

Lecture Sixteen—Transcript
Early Modern English Syntax and Grammar

Three little words. So much of English to this point has been the story of big words; of the aureate and inkhorn vocabulary terms; of the new worlds of words that came in with science and technology, with exploration and colonization; words from European and non-European languages; coinages and polysyllables that broke like waves over the shore of England.

We saw how Alexander Gil rejected this new influx of terms and he rejected it in a language redolent of metaphor and figure that we can see, I think as well, in the language of his most famous pupil, John Milton, in *Paradise Lost*.

The English language, for Gil, is "horrid" in its root sense. It is bristling with the polysyllables of loans and coinages, but there were little words as well. And the history of the English language is a history of little words. Three little words like *do;* like *will*; and like, well, not even a word, the suffix "-ing." These are forms that are so radically changing their function and their meaning in the 16th and 17th centuries that we might say that the very shape of Modern spoken idiomatic English hinges on their changes.

In this lecture, I'm going to pay attention to some very little words, and I'm going to look at some little words as changing their form and function, and I'm going to conclude with a reading of a great text—a bit of Shakespeare's play *Henry IV, Part I*, as really a play about little words.

The English of the 16th and early 17th centuries is not Modern English. True, the Great Vowel Shift had changed pronunciation from Middle English, and many of the words that were coming in—from science and exploration and from coinages and from borrowings—many of them would fill in the English vocabulary as we still have it today. But certainly in idiom, in spoken expression, in colloquialism, the language at the time of Shakespeare is not our own.

What I would like to suggest is that this very idiomatic quality of Modern spoken English is what emerges in the age of Shakespeare— the late 16th and early 17th centuries. And I want to just pause for a minute to say something about the nature of idiom itself.

When we talk about idiom, we talk about expressions that are, if you like, more than the sum of their constituent parts. So that if, for example, you were to look up the words *get* and *over, under, into, out of* in a dictionary, and try to put them together, that wouldn't tell you what expressions like *get over, get under, get into, get out of, get up on,* what these kinds of expressions mean. They are idioms in that they collocate together meanings that go beyond simply the lexical in the dictionary. It is this idiomatic quality of English that emerges at the time.

I think a large part of that idiomatic quality comes from changes in the verb *do*. *Do* has a very ancient history; it goes all the way back to Indo-European, and it appears in Old English and in Middle English, but the uses of the word change dramatically in the 16th and 17th centuries. One could argue that the tone of Modern spoken English is in many ways shaped by the way in which we use the verb *do*. In addition, the "-ing" forms are going to add to the flavor of our language. This is a suffix that also goes back to Indo-European origins that survives in the Germanic languages and that signals nouns and participles of verbs. But, the way in which it comes to be used in the 16th and 17th century gives rise to a new structure of the English verbal system.

Let's look at *do*. As a full verb, *do* means *to perform an action*—(I *did* this). This is its oldest and most sustained use, and this appears in Old English. But *do* can also be used as a replacement verb: I went to the store and having done that, I bought some eggs, or something like that. Here, the verb *do* replaces the verb *go*—that is, go/went. I went to the store and having *done* that. … In other words, we don't say, "I went to the store and having gone to the store. …" We could say that but we can also say, "Having *done* that." In other words, *do* is a replacement verb and this usage develops in the Middle English period.

What develops in the early Modern English period in the 16th century is what we call a "periphrastic," or a place-holding verb. *Do you know the way?* This is a way of asking a question, and you will remember from my previous lectures, that in Old and Middle English, and even in certain forms of early Modern English, the way you asked a question was by inverting the order of the subject and the verb in a sentence. *You know the way* is a statement. *Know you the way?* is a question.

What emerges in the 16th century is a way of asking a question by using the verb *to do* and its forms as a periphrastic, or as a place holder. So what we see also is the way in which *do* can function as an emphatic modal or helping verb. *Do you know the answer? I know the answer.* I *do* know the answer. This emphasis on *do* develops also in the 16th century. The idea *did you do it?* I *did* it. I *did do* it.

What does Othello say at that great moment in his play? "Perdition catch my soul, but I do love thee." He's able to use *do* in a new way—to emphasize the fact that he really *does* love her.

In addition to these changing forms of *do*, there were changes in the forms of "-ing." Old English had words that ended in "-ing" or "-ung" as did all the Germanic languages to indicate a noun's ownership or genealogy or to turn a verb into a noun: *Hrunting* is the name of a sword; the *Schildings* in *Beowulf* are a clan or family; and in Modern German, you use the "-ung" ending in order to signal a noun made out of a verb, or a concept noun. This is true too in Old and in Middle English. And in the Middle English period, the "-ing" forms, as participles, were used but only in southern dialects.

What do I mean by that? *Going, having*—I'm *going* to the store, or I'm *having* something, or I was *doing* something. All of these "-ing" forms as participles in the Northern and the Midland forms of English are "-ende" or "-ande"—*havande, lovande*. Lovande is the participial form of *to love*. In the south of England, you'd say *loving*, in the Midlands and the north, you'd say *lovande* or *lovende*. So this is a regional dialect form that is gradually accepted into standard English by the close of the Middle English period, and it's another product, I think, of that great migration of dialectical forms and of regional speakers into the London metropolis.

What happens in the 16th century is that some of these forms start to enter into the metropolitan standard. And so "-ing" forms develop as follows—I'll do this in the abstract. The x being y, he did this. The house, *being* on fire, he ran out. Now that is a kind of expression that you can only start to say towards the end of the 16th century, or the "x-ing of the y," like the *mowing* of the grass, the *growing* of the grain, the *lowing* of the cows. These kinds of expressions using "-ing" are idioms that do not appear until the late 16th century— expressions such as "don't blame me for having done it."

Shakespeare is really the first writer to use this form. Or, for example, new ways of expressing perfect tenses: "I have been waiting," "I had been waiting." In other words, what's going on here is the way of expressing pasts in different ways. "I have been waiting" means I began an action in the past and it continues into the present. "I had been waiting" means that I began an action in the past and continued it and it ended in the past. These are new ways of using "-ing" to signal these forms. They're also ways of expressing the future: "I am going to hit you. I am going to grade your papers. I am going to get something to eat." While this form in fact didn't appear until the late 16th century, it's really not idiomatic in English, in other words, it doesn't gain currency until the 19th.

Idiomatic Modern English, I believe, is founded on changes such as these. The point is not simply that these changes alter the way in which we speak, but that they become characteristic of the way we speak—that is, using the verbs of *do* and using forms in "-ing" are characteristic of the idiom of Modern spoken colloquial English.

While these things are going on—see, it's almost too natural to avoid—new forms of the pronouns are taking shape. Recall that there were two kinds of pronouns: you had the singular and you had the plural, and they corresponded in Old and Middle and early Modern English to that same kind of pronominal system that you see in the modern European languages where you had the informal and the formal. They were *you* for the formal and the plural, and *thee* for the informal (or the intimate) and the singular.

I want to say a little bit about the third-person pronoun. The third-person pronoun signals the neuter. Now you remember in an earlier lecture, how I had talked about how grammatical gender was beginning to disappear in the late Old English period. By the middle of the 13th century, Walter of Bibbesworth, in his treatise for aristocrats and gentry trying to learn French, has to remind them that grammatical gender is a central feature of French.

Natural gender begins to replace grammatical gender, so instead of saying "We've hit the wife, it," you would say, "The wife, she." Now what happens in the 16th and 17th centuries is that *it*, if you like, becomes a place where gender and relationships of grammar in general find themselves played out. *It* and *its*—a tiny little word—this is our notion of the third-person neuter genitive—its. This is a very late development. This is not "it"-apostrophe-"s", which is a contraction for "it is", this is *its*—*its* time, *its* person.

Even as late as Shakespeare and the King James Bible, grammatical gender can still be used. Here's a line from the *The Merchant of Venice*: "How far that little candle throws his beams!"

This is not personification—this is a grammatical throwback, if you like. It is, by this time, most likely an archaism, but it's a deliberate archaism—that is, it harkens back to a time when grammatical gender was still operating. Take this phrase from the King James Bible, "If the salt hath lost his savor"—that is, the salt has lost its taste. Again, we are not personifying salt as masculine, we're simply going back to a time when grammatical gender mattered. And so, this is not personification, it's grammar. Look at the language in flux. Again, in the time of Shakespeare, *it* and *its* hadn't fully sorted themselves out. There's a line from *King Lear* in which a character says, "That nature which condemn it origin."

We would have to say that nature which condemns *its* origin. Shakespeare is being perfectly grammatical for his own time. This is not a question of someone misspeaking. The possessive here is just *it*—it's not quite sorted out that it's *its*. So when we see these cracks and fissures in grammar, what we're looking at is a system of pronouns in transition. This is also true for comparatives and superlatives at this time.

Shakespeare can talk about a "most unkindest cut of all," and this multiplication is not ungrammatical, it's perfectly grammatical. It is the legacy of later 18th-century pedagogues who eliminate things like multiple negation and multiple comparatives and superlatives, believing that they are illogical or contradictory.

What else is happening at this time to shape the way in which we speak? There are changes in a set of verbs which we call "modal verbs," or "helping verbs." These are verbs like *shall, will, can, may, ought*, and the like. They modify the tense or mood of a main verb, but they cannot by themselves be the only verb in a sentence—that is, in Modern spoken English, they cannot take an object alone; they cannot be transitive verbs.

Originally, these verbs were full verbs. There was a time when you could say something like, "I can music." In the 17th century, you could say, "I can music," which means, "I have a certain skill and ability in music." Or, Chaucer in the 14th century could say, "I shall to God and you," meaning, "I am indebted to God and you"—I owe something to God and you. Or, in Old English, you could use *may* as a full verb and you could say, "*Ich may well*," which means "I'm in good health"—really, I may be well, but *may* is being used as a full verb.

In the 16th and the 17th centuries, these verbs were changing usage and meaning, and I want to trace some of their development. *Shall* or *should, will* and *would, may* and *might, can* and *could*—these are distinctions that arose during this period to create a subjunctive mood comparable to Latin. What does this mean? The subjunctive in Latin was used to express the counterfactual—that is, something that hadn't happened. It was also used to express what was called the optative—that is, the desire: Would that Mary would be making pies, you know, O that she would love me. This is a use of a from that is deliberately designed in the 16th and the 17th centuries to evoke a Latin grammatical category—that is, to come up with a real subjunctive in this way.

What happens is that *shall* and *will* come to be restricted for forms of the future. By the end of the 16th century, they lose their full verbal sense. So the idea of *shall* as a form of obligation, this is no longer being used, and *will* as the form of the action of an individual's will or desire in Modern spoken German, *Ich will*, means *I want*, not I will. This is being used in the King James Bible to translate *volo*— that is, the verb meaning *desire* or *volition*.

In everyday speech, what seems to be fascinating to me is the way in which this becomes something of emphasis. I remember when I was a child being taught grammar, I was taught to say that the standard non-emphatic form of expressing futurity was *I shall / you will / he will*. If you were to be emphatic about it, you were supposed to say, *I will / you shall / he shall*. Where do we draw the line between grammar and stylistic idiom here? I have no sense now that anybody in Modern spoken English makes this kind of distinction, and certainly I have to think very, very carefully about making such a distinction between *shall* and *will* as forms of emphasis.

It seems to me that what's going on here is that there is a change in the modal structure of verbs during the 16th and 17th centuries which

©2008 The Teaching Company.

up until—what shall I say—up until my own lived memory, seems to be operating. What we see in words like *do* and *shall* and *will* and forms like "-ing," what we see are changes in the structure of spoken English that make it more idiomatic than it was.

What is happening at this time is a different kind of colloquialism. But we need also to understand the relationship of this colloquialism to—how can I put it—the language of ritual. We can say things like, "How is it going?" or "How do you do?" These are relatively modern ways of expressing questions of experience. These are idioms of everyday speech, and they rely on these grammatical forms duly developed in the 16th and 17th centuries.

What about formal speech? What about ritual? I would like to close this lecture with an analysis of a wonderful moment in Shakespeare's play *Henry IV, Part I,* where the language of ritual is evoked in a new way, and where, for Shakespeare's audience of the late 16th century, the changes in forms of *do* and *will* would have been palpable and pointed. So here it is: act II, scene iv, *Henry IV, Part I.* The young Prince Hal and his old friend Falstaff are taking turns playing parts with each other. They banter back and forth and Hal says, "Do thou stand for me, and I'll play my father."

So he invites Falstaff to pretend that he is Hal and Hal will play his father, who is King Henry IV. Finally, in one of the great set pieces of this play, Falstaff, who's playing Hal, gives what may be one of the grandest self-eulogies in all of English literature. He concludes it by saying the following:

> ... but, for sweet Jack Falstaff, kind Jack Falstaff, true Jack Falstaff, valiant Jack Falstaff, and therefore more valiant, being, as he is, old Jack Falstaff, banish not him thy Harry's company, banish not him thy Harry's company. Banish plump Jack, and banish all the world.

At this moment, Hal speaking perhaps as his father or speaking as himself, utters what to my mind are the four saddest words in Shakespeare. He says, "I do, I will."

What's happening in this scene? Falstaff is making a plea for the sustained company and support from Prince Hal. He imagines himself as Prince Hal, pleading with Hal's father, King Henry IV, saying how wonderful Falstaff is, and if you banish him, you banish all the world. And what Hal says is, "I do, I will."

This play, probably written in the 1590s, uses these little words in ways that could not have been used before. For when he says, "I do," and "I will," he's using *do* now in that new sense of the replacement for Falstaff's verbs. Banish—"I do" means "I banish," but "I do" and "I will" means something else by the end of the 16th century.

In 1549, Archbishop Thomas Cranmer put together what he called the *Book of Common Prayer*. He put it together for the church under King Henry VIII's successor, Edward VI. Over the next five decades, this book, in various revisions, served as the base text for English Protestantism. Its language is familiar to us still today. And I read from the Marriage Ceremony from the *Book of Common Prayer*:

> Dearly beloved friends, we are gathered here together in the sight of God and in the face of this congregation to join together this man and this woman in holy matrimony.

At this moment, the priest is supposed to turn to the man, and he asks:

> Wilt thou have this woman to thy wedded wife? The man to answer, "I will." [And when he turns to the woman and asks the same question], she shall answer, "I will."

This moment from a Shakespeare play and this ritual from the *Book of Common Prayer* resonate, for what we see now in the marriage ritual is the affirmation of matrimony through new words used in these ways. *Do* and *will* are now the loci, if you like, of English understanding and identity. What happens at the end of this scene in Shakespeare is, I think, not a marriage, but a divorce—that Hal and Falstaff playing out this comic scene of power use these little words in deep and profound ways. These pledges now become not pledges of uniting, but pledges of separating. Hal offers up, in essence, not the rituals of marriage, but the rites of a divorce.

Shakespeare was a master of the large word and the little word. In my subsequent lectures, we're going to see how Shakespeare and so many of his contemporaries could take the new world of words, the great vocabulary of expansion, of polysyllables and polysemy, and weave it into a tapestry of the imagination.

But, as I've stressed here, we need also to look at the little words. We need to see the changes in the modal system of verbs, we need to see the changes in the forms of *do* and *will*, and we need to see the ways in which these changes radically affected the rituals of power and desire in early modern England. So I leave you with "I do", "I will"—the things that I will plan to do; the things that you will hear in later lectures.

Lecture Seventeen
Renaissance Attitudes toward Teaching English

Scope:

To a certain extent, the course thus far has tried to articulate the nature of a standard English throughout the history of the language, and to show the various ways in which standards were viewed over time. Having seen Chancery and Caxton create new institutional authorities for the standardization of English writing, we can turn now to 16th- and 17th-century developments to define the nature of English at this time and to discern contemporary attitudes toward that nature. The lecture focuses on the role of education, regionalism, and nationalism in the debate about standard English during the period, and how that debate has influenced the spelling, sound, and form of English as we speak and write it today.

Outline

I. The idea of "correct spelling" is an invention of the pedagogues and pedants of the 16th and 17th centuries. In this lecture, we'll explore issues in the teaching of spelling to learn how English spelling was regularized and to identify the ideology behind the idea of spelling "correctly."

   A. In the course of the Renaissance, an attitude toward language keyed to education emerged in the English schoolroom and university. This attitude grew out of the provocations of new vocabulary terms and changes in syntax and pronunciation that we have looked at in the past few lectures.

   B. Before considering how institutions helped to shape English, we must review the three major changes that took place in English during the period 1500–1700.

      1. The first major change we noted was the enormous increase in vocabulary—the rise of inkhorn terms and aureate diction, as well as the entrance into the language of words and coinages from science, philosophy, and technology. Contact with non-English-speaking peoples through trade and exploration also introduced new terms and provoked philosophical questions about the origins of language. The phenomenon of polysemy, in which

older words took on new meanings, sometimes figurative meanings, further contributed to the increase in English vocabulary.

2. The period from 1500 to 1700 also saw changes in syntax and grammar. By the end of this period, the major patterns of word order, word endings, and grammar would be recognizable as our own. The changes we noted in the verb *do*, the use of modal verbs as helping verbs, and the rise of verbal forms ending in "-ing" all contributed to the greater idiomatic flavor of English.

3. By 1700, the GVS had run its course, and pronunciation, with a few exceptions (some words still rhymed in the 18th century that didn't rhyme later), probably differed little from that of our own time.

C. In addition to these three major changes, the 16th and 17th centuries also saw a central change in spelling to reflect history rather than pronunciation.

1. With the emergence of Chancery in the late medieval period, scribes began to use standard spellings as opposed to spellings that reflected their regional origins.

2. William Caxton applied the official documentary standard of Chancery to literature. He respelled earlier works of Middle English literature, notably Chaucer's, when he printed them in the 1470s and 1480s.

II. The issue of spelling was a major problem for schoolmasters of the Renaissance.

A. Under the influence of teachers and scholars, literary writers and translators began to respell certain native or long-accepted loan words in new ways—ways that were not really etymological or historical but pseudo-etymological. Let's look at some examples.

1. Such words as *debt* and *doubt* came into Middle English from French forms and were never spelled with what we might call a silent "b." But these words came to be respelled to look like the Latin words *debitum* and *dubitare*. Such silent letters are the "fantasies" of schoolteachers.

2. The word *adventure* came into Middle English as *aventure* (with no "d" in the spelling), also by way of

French. The "d" was later added to reflect an imagined etymology from the Latin *ad venire*, "to enter into," "to journey into."

3. The same is true of the words *perfect* (from French *parfait*) and *verdict* (from French *voir dit*); in Middle English, neither was spelled with a "c." Both were respelled to resemble Latin.

B. Spelling became a mark not of pronunciation—or in cases such as these, not even of word history—but of learning itself. Those who could not spell well were considered illiterate. The equation of spelling with a moral or ethical, as well as an educational, level of accomplishment is the legacy of the Renaissance schoolroom.

III. If spelling represented an ideal of education, the idea of "educated speech" also emerged at this time.

A. Old criteria for a standard form of speech, such as region, class, or official affiliation, gave way to a new criterion: education, which effaced regional and class boundaries.

B. The idea that an individual's birth did not determine uniquely or irrevocably his or her class was an important change in the court and diplomatic life of Renaissance England. The result can be seen in the figure of Shakespeare, the son of a glover, who rose in society through education and verbal accomplishment.

IV. To trace this new idea and the development of a standard, let's look at some selections from Renaissance schoolmasters, theorists, and pedagogues.

A. John Hart, writing in the 1560s, represents those who focused on education as a factor. Hart considered the best English to be that of the learned and the literate, "which every reasonable English man, will the nearest he can, frame his tongue thereunto."

1. Hart's phrasing is interesting because for much of the Middle Ages, the concept of literacy was associated with an individual's command of Latin. That ability is now extended to the command of English.

2. In speaking of "every reasonable English man," Hart refers to an intellectual quality of reason. In other words,

rationality requires one to write and speak according to the standards of the learned and the literate.

3. Hart's notion of good reading and writing seems to be class-based or education-based.

B. In 1619, Alexander Gil, also focusing on education, wrote that all spelling is to be accommodated to the sound not used by "plowmen, maidservants and porters, but by learned or elegantly refined men in speaking and writing." That is, English spelling should be keyed to forms of pronunciation, and the arbiters of pronunciation should be men of the upper classes, men like Gil himself.

C. For other writers, regionalism was critical.

1. George Puttenham, writing in 1589, recommended the best English as that of the court and the region of England nearest the court, a radius of about 60 miles around London in the southeast. It's possible, Puttenham says, that some people outside this area speak Southern educated English, but the common people do not. He advocates a regional standard keyed to the locations of the institutions that arbitrate good usage (the court and universities).

2. Owen Price, writing in 1665 in *The Vocal Organ*, considered the speech of "London and our Universities" as the best standard. Interestingly, we see in Price's writing a semantic shift in the word *vulgar*; once meaning simply "of the people," by the 17th century *vulgar* had been transformed into a pejorative.

D. In the course of these debates, the issue of spelling reform also arose. Some writers advocated retaining the system of spelling historically and developing systems of pronunciation apart from spelling. Others argued that spelling should be radically reformed to represent pronunciation. Isaac Newton became so fascinated with the idea of representing speech in written form that he developed a phonetic alphabet.

1. Richard Mulcaster (1530–1611), first director of Merchant Taylor's School, was Edmund Spenser's teacher, and later head of St. Paul's School. He claimed

that English spelling was fine as it was, and advocated not reform but consistency.

   2. Alexander Gil held the opposite view, advocating a new system of spelling that would make the sound of English clear to anyone.

E. Through such writings, the "genius" ("essence") of the language became a topic of discussion that would be raised to an even higher level in the 18th century in the work of Samuel Johnson and his contemporary lexicographers and critics.

Reading:

Albert C. Baugh and Thomas M. Cable, *A History of the English Language*.

Murray Cohen, *Sensible Words: Linguistic Practice in England, 1640–1785*.

E. J. Dobson, *English Pronunciation, 1500–1700*.

M. L. Samuels, *Linguistic Evolution, with Special Reference to English*.

Questions to Consider:

1. How was English spelling influenced by the work of Renaissance schoolmasters?

2. Does English possess more "genius" than any other language?

Lecture Seventeen—Transcript
Renaissance Attitudes toward Teaching English

How many of you can spell well? I was a terrible speller as a child and still am. I think there are times when computer spell checkers are the only thing that saves me from embarrassment. The idea of spelling well is an invention of the pedagogues and pedants of the 16th and 17th centuries. The core of this lecture is going to be the idea of English spelling. And I want to look at issues in pedagogy—in teaching, that is—in spelling, not just to see how English spelling is regularized, but how, if you like, there's something of an ethos or an ideology to spelling well.

What emerges in the course of the Renaissance in the English schoolroom and the English university is an attitude towards language keyed to education. This attitude grows out of the provocations of new vocabulary terms, changes in syntax and pronunciation that I have been detailing in my previous lectures.

Before considering how the institutions helped to shape English, I want to review some of the major changes in English of the period— that is, the three major things that have been going on—and this is a good time to go back over some of the technical material that I have been outlining in my previous lectures.

You'll remember this enormous increase in vocabulary—that is, that in the period from 1500 to 1700, you see the rise of inkhorn terms; you see science, philosophy, and technology creating new words and new coinages; we have the rise of "aureate diction"—of an elaborate Latinate and romance vocabulary in poetry—and what we also have is an attitude towards language that sees English as voracious, or omnivorous, when it comes to new words.

As we will see in my subsequent lectures, Shakespeare is one of the greatest coiners of words in the English language, and some people think that he personally came up with something like 6,000 new words and added to the root stock, if you like, of the English vocabulary. Contact through trade, exploration with non-English peoples introduced new terms, but it also provoked questions about the philosophy of language—that is, what was the original language? Was there a language of Adam? Was there a language from which we had fallen? What does it mean to come in contact with the native peoples of North and South America, and recognize not simply that they have different words for things you've never seen, but recognize that the very structure, sound and pattern of their language was so alien, so different, that to some it did not seem like language at all.

Literature prompted this wider golden or aureate vocabulary, and what you also had was what I called polysemy—that is, not just a rise in the raw number of words, but the changing meaning of older words. So words from economy, words from psychology could take on figurative meanings. Words such as *flagrant* and *ardent*, that originally meant *to burn*, or be on fire were taking on emotional connotations. A word like *silly*, which originally meant *blessed*, was taking on the connotation of meaning *odd* or *unusual*. And so, what you see here is a shift in the English vocabulary system and different resources that different writers could use.

In addition to changes in vocabulary, the period from 1500 to 1700 saw changes in syntax and grammar. We've seen from my previous lectures how by about the year 1700, the major patterns of word order, of word endings, and of grammar have become recognizable as our own—that is, your standard word order pattern in a declarative sentence—subject/verb/object; the use of the verb *do* to ask a question and to create emphasis; the use of *do* as a replacement verb; the use of modal verbs: *shall, will, may, ought*, as helping verbs in the sentence; and the rise of verbal forms in "-ing": I'm *going* to do something, *having* done this, and the like. These all contribute to what I considered the greater idiomatic flavor of English during the time—that English was becoming more and more idiomatic.

Third, you have spelling and pronunciation. By about the year 1700, the Great Vowel Shift—you'll remember, the Great Vowel Shift is the change in the pronunciation of the long, stressed monophthongs of Middle English—they have pretty much changed now and the Great Vowel Shift as a systemic change in English had pretty much run its course by the year 1700. So pronunciation at the beginning of the 18th century, with a few exceptions, is probably little different from the pronunciation of our own time to two, three centuries later.

As I illustrated in some writers such as Alexander Pope, some words still rhymed in the 18th century that didn't rhyme later, and we can see in certain pockets of American regional dialect, archaic or older forms of pronunciation that remind us of a time when the Great Vowel Shift hadn't fully run its way through.

Now during this period, there is a central change in spelling. Spelling continues to reflect history rather than pronunciation. We saw that perhaps the biggest change in attitude towards spelling in the late-medieval period is the rise of Chancery—that is, the place where official documents were handwritten for the government of England, and where scribes, regardless of their regional origin, would be taught to spell in standard ways. And we looked in earlier lectures at some examples of Chancery English to indicate how spelling was gradually becoming divorced from pronunciation.

Spelling represented conventions; it did not represent pronunciation. What we saw in the work of William Caxton, England's first printer, was how Caxton respelled, in effect, the earlier works of Middle English literature—notably Chaucer—when he came to print them in the 1470s and 1480s. Caxton took an official documentary standard as a new literary standard, and through the influence of print, these forms of spelling took hold in the late 15th, 16th, and 17th centuries.

Let's look at spelling as an issue for schoolmasters in the Renaissance. Under the influence of teachers and scholars, literary writers and translators began to respell certain native or certain long-accepted loan words in new ways. So, what I would like to suggest is this: there are times when spelling is genuinely etymological. In other words, times when we still spell the word *knight*, meaning a fighter on horseback, K-N-I-G-H-T. We spell *through* T-H-R-O-U-G-H. We do not pronounce these words in this way: "knigt," and "thrauh," but our spelling maintains the history of their older pronunciation. These are, if you like, historical or etymological spellings.

In the course of the 16th and 17th century, however, the idea of historical or etymological spelling took hold with such vigor and such vehemence that certain traditionally-spelled words in English were respelled to evoke what scholars imagined to be their etymology. What I'm getting at is that there is a new concept at work: that English spelling should be historical, even if that spelling doesn't really reflect the actual history of the word. So let me give you some examples.

Take the words *debt*, which we spell D-E-B-T, and *doubt*, which we spell D-O-U-B-T. These words originally came from Latin and they entered French, but they came into Middle English from French. When they entered Middle English, the word *debt* was spelled D-E-T-T, or D-E-T-T-E, and the word *doubt* was very often spelled D-O-U-T-E. These were words which in their English spelling never had a "b" in them. But schoolmasters of the 16th and 17th centuries insisted on spelling these words with "b's" because they believed that they were ultimately descended from Latin words, and in a sort of sense they were—that is, they originally come from the Latin words *debitum* and *dubitare*—those are the Latin verbs—but they never entered English directly from Latin. They entered by way of French.

So here is an interesting question about silent letters. There are words like *knight* and words like *through* which have silent letters because we have lost their pronunciation. But there are words like *debt* and *doubt* that have silent letters, but those letters were never pronounced. The "b's" are the spelling fantasies, if you like, of schoolteachers.

Let me give you some other examples of how pedagogical and pedantic spelling reform leapfrogged, if you like, over the real history of English to go back to imagined Latin roots. Take a word like *adventure*. *Adventure* comes originally from the Latin *ad venire*—*to enter into*, or *to journey into something—to go towards*. Again, this is a word that comes into English by way of French. In Middle English the word is *aventure*—it's never *ad-venture*, it's *aventure*— but it was respelled just as *debt* and *doubt* were respelled with "b's." Here is a word that is respelled with a "d"—*adventure*— to reflect this older, imagined etymology.

Take a word like *perfect*. *Perfect, perfectus, perfectum, to make in an excellent way*, or to be an ideal of. This, again, is a word that enters Middle English from its French form, *parfait*. Chaucer's knight in the *Canterbury Tales* is *a very parfit gentil knycht*. He's a very perfect or idealized gentle knight. Throughout the Middle English and early Modern period, *perfect* was in fact spelled *parfit*. Again, it is respelled to reflect an imagined Latin origin.

And I'll give you another example: *verdict*. Yes, it's from Latin, but it comes into English from French. The way it comes into English is in the French form *voir dit*. *Verdict* means *to speak the truth*. In French *voir dire* means to speak the truth. We still use that phrase in law when we're talking about interviewing a jury, but when we talk about the result of that jury's deliberations, we talk about the *verdict*.

Chaucer's *Canterbury Tales* will have its host, Harry Bailey, set up the tale-telling game, and they will all judge which pilgrim tells the best tale. That judgment will be a *voir dire*, and that's how it's spelled in Middle English. It is a French phrase. Once again, it is respelled not as French, but as Latin by schoolmasters of the 16th and 17th centuries. *Verdict.*

How do these specific examples construct a cultural attitude? Spelling—and this is the theme of this lecture—spelling becomes a social accomplishment—that is, for the first time being a really good or really a proper speller is a mark of literacy; it is a mark of learning and education. If you do not spell well, you are considered illiterate. Our pedagogical preoccupations with good spelling, therefore, are the lineal descendants of these attitudes of Renaissance schoolmasters. The equation of spelling, indeed, with almost a kind of moral or ethical as well as educational level of accomplishment, this is the legacy of the Renaissance schoolroom.

If spelling represented an ideal of education, the idea of educated speech was also emerging at this time. You'll remember from my previous lectures how the question of a standard spoken English was very often grounded on the level of region, class, or official affiliation. In other words, was the region of West Saxony—of Wessex—was West Saxon English going to be the standard of Old English—a regional form? Was the East Midland dialect of Middle English going to become a national literary standard? Was Chancery going to become a standard? Was the language of the aristocrats going to be a standard?

Older notions of where you came from, or the stratum into which you were born, or the place where you worked, these old standards of region, class, or official affiliation give way, in the course of the 16th and 17th centuries, to a new criterion, and that criterion is education.

The idea of education was that a person from any area or any class could potentially be educated to read and write in the same way. So the new idea here is that, if you like, education effaces regional boundaries. In other words, there should come a point when, if you were well schooled enough, no one could guess where you'd come from. But also, that education trumped region or class. This is an important move in Renaissance English courtier and diplomatic life. The idea that individuals could rise in power, not completely irrespective of their birth, but that their birth did not determine uniquely or irrevocably the class that they were to aspire to.

And so what you have is you have figures like Sir Thomas Wyatt in the age of Henry VIII; you have courtiers under Queen Elizabeth; you have someone like Shakespeare, the son of a glover, who can become quite wealthy, and who through education or through verbal accomplishment, if you like, can rise in society. So this is a new idea.

In order to trace this new idea, I'd like to spend the bulk of the remainder of this lecture reading to you from some selections from Renaissance schoolmasters, theorists, writers, pedagogues, authors of textbooks. These are individuals who reflected on the notions of education, on the notions of regionalism, and on the notions of spelling that are changing at this time. They're fascinating figures and I can only give you snippets of their work.

What I want to begin with is with writers who worked on education as a factor. The first writer that I'd like to quote from is a man named John Hart, and he was writing in the 1560s. He wrote that the best English was that of, and I'm quoting him here: "The learned and the literate, which every reasonable English man will the best he can frame his tongue thereunto."

Now this is a very interesting phrase, because what he does is Hart associates learning with literacy. In other words, you go to school to become literate, and literacy now is something which almost exclusively means the ability to read and write well in the vernacular. In the Middle Ages, a *literatus* in Latin, was somebody who had skill in Latin. We saw that for a very brief period in history—maybe no more than a century—in Anglo-Saxon England, literacy could also be vernacular literacy.

For much of the Middle Ages, the concept of literacy itself—whenever you called someone "literate"—you were talking about their command of Latin. By the middle of the 16th century, that extends now to a command in English. But what's also very interesting about Hart's phrasing is the way he uses the phrase, "every reasonable English man." What he means by reasonable is not simply the casual sense of—you know, a kind of reasonable or thoughtful person—what he really means is that located in the individual, will be an intellectual quality of reason—of *ratio*. In other words, that the rational thing to do here is to write and speak according to the standards of the learned and the literate.

And so what Hart does in the course of his work, in fact, is he develops a notion of good reading and writing—a notion of good English that will seem to us to be class-based or education-based, or key to certain forms of pronunciation or spelling—but he's arguing that it is the rational way to speak and read.

I'd mentioned Alexander Gil in a previous lecture. He was Milton's teacher and in 1619, he published his exceedingly important book: the *Logonomia Anglica* (*The English Language*) and he wrote it in Latin. I've given you come quotations from Gil before; I want to return to Gil now.

Gil talked about how education was very important. Here is Gil in an English translation of his Latin. He says, that, "In manners, the opinion of the good, so in pronunciation, the custom of the learned is to be taken as a basis."

So let me pause here. That is, good manners are arbitrated by good people, so good pronunciation should be arbitrated by educated people. I'll continue:

> All spelling is to be accommodated to the sound not used by plowmen, maid servants and porters, but by learned or elegantly refined men in speaking and reading.

Again, a wonderful bit of overstatement on the part of Gil. Gil is a genius, if you like, of this kind of exaggeration. But what I love here is the way in which he's talking about English spelling—that it should be keyed to forms of pronunciation and that the arbiters of pronunciation should be learned and elegantly refined men—obviously, people like Alexander Gil.

For others, regionalism was an issue. One of the most influential of writers in the Elizabethan period—that is, the last decades of the 16th century—was a man named George Puttenham. And George Puttenham, writing in 1589, recommended the best English as that of the court and the region of England nearest to the court—that is, the southeast. Here he is writing in 1589. He says, the best English, and I quote, "is the usual speech of the court and that of London, and the shires lying about London with 60 miles and not much above."

So it's almost as if what he does is he takes a map of England and he sets a compass to a 60-mile radius and puts the point right at the English court and draws the circle around. And he goes on:

> I say not this, but that in every shire of England there are gentlemen and others that speak but especially write as good southern English as we of Middlesex or Surrey do. But not the common people of every shire to whom the gentlemen and also their learned clerks do for the most part condescend.

So what he's saying is this: southern regional educated English—the language of the court and the language of the universities (and the fact is that Oxford and Cambridge are just about 60 miles from London, so that's your periphery of your radius of good speech)—that the home counties and the universities—these are the loci of good speech. And he says it's perfectly possible that there are people elsewhere in England who speak good southern English as well as anybody from this region might, but it's the common people who do not.

So what Puttenham is arguing for is a notion of a regional standard keyed to the fact that at that region, you have the institutions that arbitrate good behavior and good education.

Let me turn to someone writing about 100 years later—Owen Price—who's writing in the middle of the 17th century, in his 1665 book called *The Vocal Organ*. He writes that in his book, "I have not been guided by our vulgar pronunciation, but by that of London and our universities where the language is purely spoken."

Once again, you have a notion of region keyed to the institutions of that region, and what we also have is a very interesting shift, if you like, semantically in the word *vulgar*—the *vulgus*, *vulgar*, the *vulgi*, that was simply the word for the populace. Vulgar Latin was not dirty Latin, it was the spoken Latin. The Vulgate Bible was the version of the Latin Bible prepared in late antiquity into, if you like, the Latin of everyday speech.

By the 17th century, the word *vulgar* is being transformed into a pejorative—that is, it's not simply common or everyday, but it's now carrying with it the connotation of coarse and potentially of socially unacceptable.

In the course of this period and in the course of these debates, a larger question was arising. Should English spelling in fact be reformed? Some people argued that we should simply keep the system of spelling historically, and that we should develop systems of pronunciation that are, in effect, apart from that spelling system. In other words, that we shouldn't spell as we speak.

Others argued that we should radically reform spelling to represent pronunciation. Some writers of the 16th and 17th centuries, including in fact the scientist and natural philosopher Isaac Newton, became so fascinated with the idea of being able to represent speech in written form that they developed what we might call phonetic alphabets.

Those are the two poles of argument during the period from about the middle of the 16th, to the end of the 17th century. I want to conclude with two quotations. I want to quote to you from the writings of Richard Mulcaster who lived from about 1530 to 1611. He was the first director of the Merchant Taylor's School. He was the teacher of the poet Edmund Spenser. He was later the head of St. Paul's school. And he claimed that English spelling was fine as it was.

What he wanted was not reform but consistency, and writing in the 1590s, he's responding to spelling reformers by saying that such reforms

> … cumber our tung, both with strange caracts and with needless diphthongs. … If there want distinction, then accent must be meant to avoid confusion, or some such device, which may distinguish with praise, and not pester the writing, with any too odd strangeness."

What he's saying is this, "Look. Spelling is fine as it is and if there are some problems, then we can put in diacritical marks or we can tweak spelling a little bit, but we don't want to encumber our tongue with strange characters, with weird letter forms, and with needless diphthongs—that is, with elaborate respellings of vowels. Let's not get confused here. Let's be rational."

Alexander Gil, again, weighed in, of course, on spelling, as he weighed in on everything. His remarks on spelling with which I will conclude this lecture are really more remarks on language as a whole. It's a somewhat extended passage that I'm going to read now:

> For nothing so much contributes to the fame of a people as their language, not skill in warfare, not knowledge of literature, for through language these things are made known amongst to people, bequeathed to foreigners and handed down to posterity. For none of the languages now spoken by men will be found to be more graceful, elegant or apt for the expression of every subtle thought, than English. Admittedly, numerous faults which impede the studies of our youth have crept into our language, but by bringing back those characters used by our forefathers in antiquity, neglected through indifference in former times, and by introducing one or two new ones, I have so restored them all that any inexperienced person will be able, immediately, to perceive at first sight the proper sound of our words.

Gil develops a system of spelling with some new characters and he develops a system of spelling that is designed to make the sound of English clear to anyone. But this is more than just a statement about spelling; it's a statement about what Gil and some of his contemporaries believed to be the essence of English. What is this genius or essence of the English language?

These debates raised to a higher level in the 18th century will be debates that we will see in the work of Samuel Johnson and his contemporary lexicographers and critics. But for now, let's go back to Gil and let's go back to that time when we see not just the schoolmasters, but the playwrights on the stage.

In my next two lectures, I'm going to look closely at the work of Shakespeare to see how he reached into the wellsprings of English and bequeathed to later readers and writers something which they invariably thought of as the genius of their time.

Lecture Eighteen
Shakespeare—Drama, Grammar, Pronunciation

Scope:

This is the first of two lectures devoted to the language of Shakespeare. In both, we will see how Shakespeare deploys the lexical, grammatical, and sonic resources of his language, while offering some newer usages that, by virtue of his subsequent authority in English literature, have become acceptable. Much of Shakespeare seems modern and familiar to us, but a great deal seems old-fashioned. How does Shakespeare stand on the cusp of language change, and how does he fashion a literary language out of the fluid body of linguistic elements available at this time? Our central text for this lecture will be a short selection from the play *Richard III* that raises some important questions about pronunciation and grammatical usage at the time.

Outline

I. Shakespeare was the canonical writer of the English language. He is believed to have contributed, perhaps more than any other writer, new words and idioms to English; he created character and concept; and in his plays and poems, he gave birth to what many believe to be the first modern individuals on the stage or in the fictional imagination.

    A. In this lecture and the next one, we'll look in detail at some features of Shakespeare's language; in particular, how it might have sounded to his contemporaries, what his lexical resources may have been, and what grammatical features existed uniquely in his time that separate his language from our own.

    B. We'll also talk about the contexts in which Shakespeare's work comes down to us, such as on the stage and in the world of performance; in rhetoric and the habits of schoolroom education; and in printing, typesetting, and bookselling.

II. Shakespeare employed the language of an educated professional, at least up through the grammar school level. He was clearly well read and conversant in the ideas of the age, both scientific and literary.

A. Shakespeare did not have a university-level education, but it seems clear from his plays and poems that he knew the great works of history; the work of his own English literary forebears, including Chaucer and Spenser; and the works of Plutarch and Seneca.

B. Shakespeare can be read as a textbook on various subjects of the late 16th and early 17th centuries. His phrase "humorous night," for example, accords with the theory of humors in Renaissance psychology. In *The Tempest*, he takes his audience to "the Far Bermoothes," that is, Bermuda, a place only recently visited at the beginning of the 17th century.

C. We're familiar with any number of quotations from Shakespeare, but there are some aspects of his work that may seem unfamiliar or alien.

    1. Using the resources of historical linguistics, the sound of Shakespeare's language has been reconstructed. Given that the GVS had not completely run its course in the 17th century, certain vowel sounds would not be pronounced as they are in Modern English.

    2. The rise in usage of forms of the verb *do* and "-ing" endings, together with changes in the system of modal verbs, adjustments in syntax and word order, and the increase in the idioms of everyday English, as we have seen, had a great impact on Shakespeare's language. Nonetheless, there are many aspects of his grammar that may strike us as archaic.

        a. He used, for example, multiple negatives and comparatives: "The most unkindest cut of all."

        b. He used the third-person neuter pronoun, *it* and *its*, in distinctive ways.

        c. He used older endings for the second-person and third-person singular forms of verbs ("-st," "thou doest"; "-th," "he doth").

        d. He used two different pronouns for the second person: *thou* forms for the singular and informal and *you* forms for the plural and formal.

D. Shakespeare deployed the growing resources of his vocabulary to increase markedly the lexical basis of literary English.

  1. Many of his words came from commerce and trade, and many were coinages. At the same time, we see frequent metaphorical or figurative uses of words of technical meaning in Shakespeare's poetry and plays.

  2. In some cases, Shakespeare's words display a functional shift in their employment as different parts of speech. For example, the noun *spaniel* becomes a verb in the following line: "The harts that spanieled me at heels." In this, Shakespeare bequeaths to later writers the idea of poetic use of the language.

  3. Shakespeare also left a legacy of memorable and outstanding cursing. We see in a passage from *King Lear* his origination of the phrase *lily-livered*.

E. Shakespeare and his contemporaries would have been trained in the arts of rhetoric and oratory in school. Rhetoric is the disciplined and creative use of words for the purposes of persuasion. The job of the rhetorician was to evoke an emotional response in the listener or reader.

  1. We earlier referred to Thomas Wilson's *Art of Rhetoric*, one of the first major textbooks in the middle of the 16th century that dealt with ways of organizing speech according to formal models for poets, courtiers, orators, and writers.

  2. When we look at Shakespeare's poetry, especially the sonnets and the soliloquies in the plays, we can readily see these patterns of rhetorical organization.

III. Let's now turn to a passage from *Richard III*, act I, scene ii, to examine these features of Shakespeare's language in action.

  A. In this passage, Lady Anne is going to the funeral of her father-in-law, Henry VI, when she meets Richard, who has murdered both the old king and Lady Anne's husband. Richard and Anne argue, and the passage calls attention to several important issues relating to sound and sense.

  B. In listening to the passage read with a late-16th-century pronunciation, we note again that the GVS was not complete.

1. The Middle English long, high vowels /u/ and /i/ had not yet become the modern diphthongs /au/ and /ai/. Thus, *thou* and *my* would have been pronounced "tho" and "moy."
2. The Middle English long vowel /o/ had not fully moved up to its modern position /i/. The word *undertake* would have been pronounced "oondertaak."
3. Some words, such as *cause* and *haunt*, were probably still pronounced as they had been in Middle English: "cowse" and "hount."
4. The pronunciation of other words, such as *world* and *Mary/merry/marry*, is more difficult to pin down, because the sounds of the letters "w" and "r" affect the pronunciation of vowels that follow them. This instability in pronunciation is reflected in Modern English in such words as *person/parson*, *vermin/varmint*, and *university/ varsity*, which share the same roots.

C. The passage from Richard III can be read as an essay in second-person forms. The heart of its drama is the interchange of *thou* and *you* forms, signaling the shifting personal relationship between Richard and Anne.
  1. Richard is trying to woo Anne, but she spurns him. She opens the scene with a contemptuous and condescending *thou*, as if Richard were a servant. Richard responds with a socially correct and formal *you*.
  2. In the final line, however, when Richard seeks to make clear that he wants her sexually, he calls Anne *thee*.
  3. In this passage, Shakespeare manipulates resources of the language that are now lost to us. Here is the paradox of Shakespeare for modern readers: The sound and grammar of his language seem transparent to us, but they still hinge on particular details of his time and place.

IV. In addition to the contexts of grammar, vocabulary, and pronunciation, another important context for understanding Shakespeare is that of print, where we find many surprises.

A. The passage we just read can be found in the First Folio edition of Shakespeare's plays. In this book, published in 1623, we find the texts of almost all the plays, but 17th-century printing, especially of drama, was a very different enterprise from modern publication. For example, Shakespeare's plays circulated in various versions before the First Folio printing, including as actors' copies (the *quarto* texts) and pirated editions.

B. Some aspects of the visual appearance of Shakespeare's early printed texts seem to alienate us from the author.

   1. Almost all readers, for example, have noted the similar appearance of the letters "f" and "s," but close inspection reveals that the two letters are written differently.

   2. In some early editions, the word *that* appears to be written as a "y" followed by a superscripted "t" (y^t). This appearance is a holdover from the earlier borrowing of a letter from the runic alphabet (the thorn—þ) to represent the interdental sound "th."

C. In our next lecture, we'll look at some of the ways in which the stage and the page work in tandem and in tension to give us a Shakespeare who is, at once, remarkably familiar and radically alien.

Reading:

Paul Bertram and Bernice W. Kliman, eds., *The Three-Text Hamlet*.

Charlton Hinman, ed., *The Norton Facsimile: The First Folio of Shakespeare*.

Frank Kermode, *Shakespeare's Language*.

Stephen Orgel and A. R. Braunmiller, *The Pelican Shakespeare*.

Questions to Consider:

1. How does Shakespeare's language reflect the evolving state of Early Modern English?

2. Was the role of rhetoric in Renaissance education greater than it is today?

Lecture Eighteen—Transcript
Shakespeare—Drama, Grammar, Pronunciation

Shakespeare. The very name evokes the acme of the English language. Shakespeare, perhaps more than any other writer contributed, it is believed, new words and idioms to English; he created character and concept; and in his plays and poems, he gave rise to what many believe to be the first modern individuals on the stage or in the fictional imagination.

Shakespeare's presence in the history of the English language is unquestionably important. What I would like to do in this and in my following lecture is to look in detail at some features of Shakespeare's language—in particular, how it might have sounded to his contemporaries; what the nature of his lexical resources may have been—that is, what his vocabulary was—what grammatical features existed uniquely in the time of Shakespeare and separate that language from our own.

But what I'd also like to talk about are some of the contexts in which Shakespeare's work comes down to us. Such contexts include the stage and habits of performance; rhetoric and the habits of schoolroom education; and printing and the habits of typesetting, book selling, and book marketing that present the Shakespearean text in a form that visually may seem very alien to us today.

Shakespeare was in many ways *the* canonical writer in English, but how much can we attribute to him? He employed the language of an educated professional—that is, at least up through the grammar school level. He's clearly very well-read and conversant in the ideas of the age, both scientific and literary. His contemporary, Ben Jonson, in a famous line, considered Shakespeare to have had, as he put it, "… small Latin and less Greek."

Shakespeare did not have a university-level education, but it seems clear from the basis of his plays and his poems that he knew the great works of history, that he knew his English literary forebears such as Chaucer and Spenser, that he knew the work of Plutarch and Roman and Greek history, and that he knew the plays of the Roman tragedian Seneca, whether he knew them in Latin or in their Elizabethan translations. Shakespeare was very much aware of his somewhat older contemporary Edmund Spenser, the author of *The*

Faerie Queene, and he's clearly in tune with many of the social, economic and political developments of his time.

Shakespeare can be read, if you like, as a textbook writer on various subjects of the late 16th and early 17th century. For example, you can read him as a textbook in science. He has a phrase in one of his plays, "humorous night." Now, "humorous night" does not mean funny or witty night, but night that is wet or dewy—that is, filled with something like the liquid humors that in Renaissance psychology were made up of the humors: blood and bile and sweat. These humors, or these forms of experience and feeling took liquid shape. So "humorous night" means it's kind of wet or kind of dewy.

Or a phrase such as, "the elements so mixed in him." The idea here is that the elements are the four great elements. He doesn't mean iron and aluminum and oxygen; he means earth, air, fire, and water—that is, the elements of old alchemy. So Shakespeare is a textbook of the world. We have the details of London life. We go to the forest of Arden. We go to *The Tempest*, to the land of what is called "the Far Bermoothes"—that is, the island of Bermuda—a place only recently visited at the beginning of the 17th century.

There is a famous anecdote about a playgoer in the modern period who goes to see a Shakespeare play and when he's asked about it, he says, "Well, it was okay but it was full of quotations." Shakespeare's plays are full of quotations not simply in the sense that we have quoted Shakespeare so much that many of the lines seem as if they're just quotations or clichés, but Shakespeare is full of quotations from other earlier authors—from his sources. He's full of quotations because we cannot but hear phrases that are Shakespearian in origin and that now seem memorable.

One of the questions I want to ask in this and in my subsequent lecture is what makes a phrase memorable? Why is it that Shakespeare seems to us a tissue of quotations? Before exploring the familiar Shakespeare, however, I want to say something about how he's unfamiliar or alien.

You will recall how by the 17th century, the Great Vowel Shift had not fully or completely run its course. We can use the resources of historical linguistics to reconstruct something of the sound of Shakespeare's language. Grammatically—that is, when we look at grammar and morphology—what we see are some uses that, to us, are only dimly familiar. Now you'll remember from my earlier lectures that I talked about the rise in usage of forms of the verb *do* and "-ing" endings, together with changes in the system of modal verbs, adjustments of syntax and word order, and the increase in the idioms of everyday English. These had a great impact on Shakespeare's language, but also Shakespeare's appropriation of some of these newer idioms had an impact on their later usage.

There are, however, many things about Shakespeare's grammar that may strike us as archaic. For example, he employed the use of multiple negatives and comparatives, "the most unkindest cut of all," is perhaps one of the most famous. He used the third-person neuter pronoun *it* and *its* in distinctive ways, and I called attention to some of those ways in earlier lectures. And he used older endings for the second-person singular forms of verbs, like thou *doest* and the third-person singular, he *doth*.

Shakespeare also, with varying degrees of consistency, used two different pronouns for the second person. And you will remember once again, *thou* forms that are singular and informal and *you* forms that are plural and formal. In the second part of this lecture, I'm going to go into great detail by looking at a passage from the play *Richard III*, which we could see, in effect, as a kind of drama of the second-person pronoun.

When it comes to vocabulary, of if you like, "lexis," Shakespeare deployed the growing resources of the English vocabulary to increase markedly the lexical basis of the literary language. What do we mean by this? Many of his words come from commerce and trade; many of them coinages; but many of them, too, represent metaphorical or figurative uses of words or technical meaning. Some display what we might call also a functional shift in their employment as different parts of speech, and I want to pause to give a couple of examples of this.

One idea of poetry, if you like, that I think many of us have and that I think Shakespeare develops to its acme, is the idea that you take a word from one grammatical category and you put it in another grammatical category. In other words, you take a noun and you turn it into a verb. Let me give you an example from a line of Shakespeare, "the harts that spanieled me at heels."

That is, the hart—that is, the deer—that followed me at my heels like a spaniel. If any of you have had a dog or if any of you have had a spaniel, you'll know how that spaniel follows the master at the heel, sort of breathlessly, tongue hanging out. So *to spaniel*, Shakespeare imagines, as a verb meaning *to follow like a spaniel*.

When Shakespeare does this, he shows us, I think, a new category of poetic language. In other words, Shakespeare bequeaths to later writers not simply a set of words or idioms or phrases, I think he bequeaths to later literary writers an idea of what constitutes the poetic or the literary. In other words, make nouns into verbs, make verbs into nouns, make certain compounds into adjectives.

So when we read a poet like—let me think—Dylan Thomas, for example, and we come across a line like "the heron/Priested shore" where he's describing a beach or a shoreline full of herons and they seem to be holding sway over the beach like priests, so it is a "heron/Priested shore." What you see here is an example of the kind of verbal functional shifting that Shakespeare developed to a high art.

Shakespeare gave us an idea of the poetic and the elevated, but he also gave us an idea of the vulgar and the crude. No one curses as greatly as Shakespeare; no one disses like the bard. Here's a little example from the play *King Lear*, when Kent confronts the self-important steward. And Kent describes him, and I quote, as:

> A knave, a rascal, an eater of broken meats; a base, proud, shallow, beggarly, three-suited, hundred-pound, filthy worsted-stocking knave; a lily-livered, action-taking [knave, a] whoreson, glass-gazing, superserviceable, rogue; one-trunk-inheriting slave.

What is amazing about this passage is not just its string of curses but that wonderful phrase, "lily-livered." We think of "lily-livered" as the language of the saloon rather than the language of the salon. We think of lily-livered as up there with varmint and buckaroo—a lily-livered cowpoke. But lily-livered is a Shakespearian coinage. The genius of that coinage sets itself irrevocably into the matrix of the English language. Shakespeare is a master of rhetoric.

Rhetoric in his time was the training of the school. Shakespeare and his contemporaries would have been trained in the arts of rhetoric and oratory. Rhetoric is the disciplined and creative use of words for the purposes of persuasion. The job of the rhetorician was to evoke an emotional response in the listener or in the reader. I quoted from Thomas Wilson's *Art of Rhetoric* in an earlier lecture. This was one of the first major textbooks of the middle of the 16th century that dealt with ways of organizing speech according to formal models— schemes, tropes, metaphors, images that poets and courtiers and orators and writers could use. They were all available in these ways.

Rhetoric is the art of organizing language in these special ways, and this was the job of the schoolroom. So when we look at Shakespeare's poetry, especially in the sonnets and in the soliloquies of the plays, we're going to be looking at patterns of rhetorical organization.

What I'd like to do now is I'd like to turn to an extended passage to illustrate how Shakespeare uses the resources of his language for particular dramatic effect. The passage that I'm going to focus on is a scene in *Richard III*. It is the scene between Richard and the woman that he craves, Lady Anne. Richard is interrupting Lady Anne on her way to Henry VI's funeral. This is the setup: Lady Anne had been married to Henry VI's son, Edward, and Richard had had him murdered.

So Richard raises the question of just what caused the deaths—that is, the death of Edward, but also the death of Henry VI—and Anne shoots back. And I'm just going to read it in modern pronunciation and I'm going to signal the speaker at the beginning of each line or each section.

Anne says:

> Thou wast the cause, and most accursed effect.

Richard says:

> Your beauty was the cause of that effect;
> Your beauty that did haunt me in my sleep.
> To undertake the death of all the world,
> So I might live one hour in your sweet bosom.

Anne responds:

> If I thought that, I tell thee, homicide,
> These nails should rent that beauty from my cheeks.

Richard:

> These eyes could not endure that beauty's wrack;
> You should not blemish it if I stood by;
> As all the world is cheered by the sun,
> So I by that. It is my day, my life.

Anne:

> Black night o'er shade thy day, and death thy life!

Richard:

> Curse not thyself, fair creature—thou art both.

Anne:

> I would I were, to be revenged on thee.

Richard:

> It is a quarrel most unnatural,
> To be revenged on him that loveth thee.

This is an immensely powerful passage and I want to focus on several aspects of its sense and of its sound. But first, let me reread the opening few lines in a historical reconstruction of Shakespearian pronunciation—that is, what these lines might have sounded like to Shakespeare's audience. I'm going to read the first five lines of the speech I just read. "Thoo wast the cowse and most accursed effect. Your beauty was the cowse of that effect. Your beauty that it hount me in moy sleep to oondertaak the death of all the world so oy might live un oor in your sweet bosom."

The most important thing to notice about the sound here is that the Great Vowel Shift had not sorted itself out as fully. When I read it aloud, what I tried to stress was that the older Middle English long, high vowels /u/ and /i/ had not completely turned into the modern diphthongs /au/ and /ai/. And so *thou* and *my* I pronounced like "tho" and "moy." So too, the older Middle English long vowel /o/ ("aw") had not fully moved up to its modern position /ai/. So what you have is a word like *undertake*, which I pronounced more like "oondertaak."

These sound changes would have distinguished Shakespeare's English from Chaucer's, but some words were probably still pronounced as they'd been in Middle English. The words *cause* and *haunt*, scholars believe, probably were still pronounced, "cowse" and "hount," as they had been in Middle English.

Some words are harder to place, and I want to go through this in a little bit of detail here. The word *world* may not have been pronounced with its old Middle English vowel, "worold," or it may have been pronounced "world." The "w-" changes the way in which you pronounce a following vowel. It rounds the form. So, very often, just to pause on "w-," you can say things like *car*, but "woar"—that is, the "w-" rounds your mouth and gets you ready and rounds the vowel. But this is also a historical change, so it's unclear whether in Shakespeare's time these "w's" were actually rounding the vowels—"world" or "worold" or something like that.

Also, the letter "r" also affected the pronunciation of sounds. Depending on where you're from these days, you may say the name *Mary*, M-A-R-Y, you may say the word *merry*, M-E-R-R-Y, and you may say the verb *to marry*, M-A-R-R-Y all completely differently, or you may say them the same—"Mary, merry, and marry"; or "Maery, merry, and meri"; or "merry, merry, and marry." The spoken English of the 16th and the 17th centuries similarly had what we might call an instability of pronunciation of words that were "-er" or "-ir" spellings.

This instability is still reflected in some forms of Modern spoken English. The word *person* and the word *parson* come from the same root. The words *vermin* and *varmint* come from the same root. The words *university* and *varsity* come from the same root. In England, you're a "clark," but in America, you are a "clerk." In America, you go to "Berkeley," and in England, you had Bishop "Barclay." These are some features of Shakespearian pronunciation that I'm trying to call attention to and that I'm trying to evoke in, if you like, my representation of the sound.

What I'd also like to talk about is the way in which this particular passage is an essay in the second-person forms. The entire passage has at its heart the drama of the interchange of *thou* and *you* forms, signaling the shifting personal relationships between Richard and Anne. Richard is trying to woo Anne. She is spurning him. She opens with a contemptuous and condescending *thou*: "Thou wast the cause." She's talking down to him, like a servant. Richard responds

©2008 The Teaching Company.

with a socially correct and formal *you*, indicating that he is directing a superior: "Your beauty."

Anne and Richard, in the course of the passage I read, exchange *thou* forms and *you* forms—she "thou's" him, and he "you's" her. But in the final line of the passage when Richard really wants to make it clear that he wants her sexually, he calls her *thee* when he says, "It is a quarrel most unnatural to be revenged on him that loveth thee." When you love, you love in the second-person informal. You love in the *thou* form.

You can see how Shakespeare, in this passage, is manipulating the resources of the language that are lost to us. One must be acutely sensitive to these shifts in pronouns and in grammar. This is the point I'm trying to make also about the paradox of Shakespeare—that he seems so modern, but he can be so alien; that the sounds, even though they're certainly not Middle English sounds, are really not Modern English sounds, and that his grammar, transparent though it may be to us, still hinges on particular details. Here, as I've suggested in this extended reading, they are the details of the second person.

In addition to the contexts of grammar, vocabulary, pronunciation, another important context for understanding Shakespeare is the context of print. Now Shakespeare in print offers many surprises. The passage that I've been talking about from *Richard III* can be found in the so-called First Folio edition of Shakespeare's plays. This book, which was published in 1623, contains just about all of his play texts. But 17th-century printing, especially of drama, was a very different enterprise than modern publication.

Many of Shakespeare's plays circulated before that posthumous First Folio printing. They circulated in different prints, maybe from actors' copies, maybe pirated editions. These were smaller books called "Quartos." And in my next lecture, I'm going to spend some time talking about Hamlet and the way in which Hamlet appears differently in the major Folio edition and in the earlier Quarto editions.

What I would like to do now is go back to the passage from *Richard III*, and talk about how it appears in the First Folio. In other words, what is there visually about the look of Shakespeare's early printed text that alienates us from Shakespeare, that locates him historically, and that helps explain some issues and resolve some problems that many of us have in looking at early print.

Let me begin with one of the most frequently asked questions that I get as a teacher of English, as a historian of language, as a scholar of the book. People will invariably say to me, "How come back in the old days, people wrote their 's's' like they were 'f's'?" It's not true. When you look at this passage in the First Folio, and when you look at any early printed book—a book printed probably before the middle of the 18th century—you have various forms of the letters. One of these is the so-called "long s" ["ʃ"]—that is, it's a long letter and it sometimes looks like an "f ["ƒ"]." But the "f" has a little crossbar and the "s" does not.

When you look closely at the text, you'll see that the "s" and the "f" are different. So, answer number one, people did not write their "s's" and "f's" in the same way.

Question number two: When you look at this passage in the First Folio, and when you look at many early printed editions, what you find is the word *that*, T-H-A-T, often abbreviated as it is here in the line, "*Theſe eyes could not endure y^t beauties wrack*." The way it looks on the printed page is it looks like a "y" and then a tiny "t" superscripted over it. This is not *it*, or *yit*, or *yet*, it's *that*. In order to explain why it's *that*, I need to tell you a little story.

In Old English and in Middle English and in early Modern English, the sound represented by our modern spelling "th" was represented by an older letter that had descended from the Runic alphabet. Runes was the system of writing that the ancient Germanic peoples had used. Runic letters were adapted by Old English scribes to represent sounds in English that did not exist in Latin. One of these sounds was the interdental continuit—remember articulatory phonetics—the inter-dental continuant "th," as in *the* and *that*.

The thorn [þ]was a letter that looked like a big "p" with a flag on it, or it looked like a "p" with a taller mast. As this came to be written very, very quickly, the bowl of the "p" gradually changed, and the top started flattening out, so that by the 15th century, when scribes were writing and when printers began to print, this "p" with a flag on it started to look more like a "y" with a hat—that is, it looked like a "y" but with the top of the "y" closed off.

Gradually, printers maintained this as a convention, and they would use the "y" to indicate, in certain abbreviations, the sound "th-." So very often, you will see in early printed books, *that* [y^t] looks like y^t. It's not. It's the descendent of the old thorn, "th" with the abbreviation. So "th-," *that*. Sometimes you'll see the definite article look like "ye." It is not.

The hallmark of the cute is Ye Olde Shoppe—Ye Olde Tavern. The definite article in English was never *ye*, it was *the*. The "y" is a printing convention that descends from the manuscript tradition of writing a "th-" sound using the old Runic letter thorn. Over time, the shape of that letter changed and it looked like a "y." So if anybody asks you, it was never "Ye Olde Shoppe."

The look of Shakespeare in his time is as different as the sound of Shakespeare in his time. And so, what we need to see in understanding Shakespeare's place in the history of the language is his relationship to speech sound, to grammar, to vocabulary, and to print culture. In my next lecture, I'm going to look at some of the ways in which the stage and the page work in tandem and in tension to give us a Shakespeare that may be remarkably familiar, but also one that is radically alien.

In the so-called Bad Quarto of *Hamlet*, we may see things that today we may not simply let be but which we would rather not be at all.

Lecture Nineteen
Shakespeare—Poetry, Sound, Sense

Scope:

Continuing from the previous lecture, we examine some texts that illustrate the verbal resources of Shakespeare's language and the changing nature of the English literary vocabulary. But we will also look at some texts that challenge our assumptions about that language and about Shakespeare's work itself. The study of the history of the language can help us untangle some of our presuppositions about what is "good" and "bad" Shakespeare and what may or not be representative texts of his work.

Outline

I. The medium of print was flexible in the Renaissance, almost as variable as writing itself. Books were often proofread in the course of production, and individual texts might be corrected or left uncorrected. Shakespeare's plays and poems are documents of Renaissance bookmaking and, as such, reflect the variations of the print shop from the stage or the mind of the author.

> To be, or not to be: that is the question:
> Whether 'tis nobler in the mind to suffer
> The slings and arrows of outrageous fortune,
> Or to take arms against a sea of troubles,
> And by opposing end them? To die: to sleep;
> No more; and by a sleep to say we end
> The heart-ache and thousand natural shocks
> That flesh is heir to, 'tis a consummation
> Devoutly to be wish'd. To die, to sleep:
> To sleep: perchance to dream: ay, there's the rub;
> For in that sleep of death what dreams may come
> When we have shuffled off this mortal coil,
> Must give us pause.

   A. *Hamlet*, one of Shakespeare's most famous and distinctive plays, comes down to us in several versions, including that in the First Folio (1623) and two earlier quarto versions.

1. The First Quarto was printed in 1603. In it, *Hamlet* is short and seems garbled, the language is remarkably different, and much of the structure and idiom of the play are almost unrecognizable.
2. The Second Quarto was printed in 1604. In this version, the speeches, the organization of the play, and the arc of the tragedy are far more familiar to us. Most modern editions of *Hamlet* are based on the Second Quarto and the First Folio.

B. In this lecture, we'll look at what is perhaps the most famous speech in all of English literature, Hamlet's "To be, or not to be" soliloquy.

II. The familiar lines of this speech give us the sense and shape of Shakespeare's rhetoric.

A. In the medieval and Renaissance schoolroom, posing problems or presenting questions to students was one approach to education. A topic of debate would be presented, and students would be expected to argue one side or the other.
1. In this soliloquy, Shakespeare removes this approach from the schoolroom and transforms it into an inner discussion in which Hamlet takes both sides of the question.
2. Shakespeare also uses extended metaphors and figurative forms that he would have learned from rhetorical manuals of the time.

B. Hamlet's soliloquy works through *anaphora*, that is, the repetition of an initial word or phrase at the beginning of a line, a sentence, or a clause. We note, for example, the repetition of the phrase "To die, to sleep." Keep in mind that Shakespeare was writing in unrhymed iambic pentameter. The anaphora fits into the metrical scheme of the speech.

C. In comparison, the First Quarto text of the speech seems garbled, improvised, and far more colloquial, without the precision of anaphora and balance.

D. Notice also the use of enjambment in the "good" version of the soliloquy. "Enjambment" is the technique of allowing a line to run on so that the end of a line is not the end of a sentence. Many people believe that enjambment is the mark of sophisticated poetry. In the "bad" version of the soliloquy, almost every line ends with the end of a clause or a sentence. The result is a sequence of broken-up lines rather than a flow of sentences.

1. Compare, for example, "To Die, to sleepe, is that all?" in the First Quarto with "To die, to sleep; to sleep: perchance to dream" in the First Folio. The first line seems like a colloquialism.

2. The phrase "For in that sleep of death, what dreams may come" (First Folio) seems far more poetic and imaginative than "For in that sleepe of death, when wee awake."

E. The First Quarto uses some phrasings that were relatively new to colloquial English in the late 16th and early 17th centuries. For example, "The widow being oppressed" makes use of the new "-ing" form that would become characteristic of idiomatic spoken English.

> To be, or not to be, I there's the point,
> To Die, to sleepe, is that all? I all:
> No, to sleepe, to dreame, I mary there it goes,
> For in that sleepe of death, when wee awake,
> And borne before an euerlasting Iudge,
> From whence no passenger euer retur'nd,
> The vndiscouered country, at whose sight
> The happy smile, and the accursed damn'd.
> But for this, the ioyfull hope of this,
> Whol'd beare the scornes and flattery of the world,
> Scorned by the right rich, the rich curssed of the poore?
> The widow being oppressed, the orphan wrong'd,
> The taste of hunger, or a tirants raigne,
> And a thousand more calamities besides,
> To grunt and sweate vnder this weary life,
> When that he may his full Quietus make,
> With a bare bodkin, who would this indure,
> But for a hope of something after death?
> Which pusles the braine, and doth confound the sence,
> Which makes vs rather beare those euilles we haue,
> Than flie to others that we know not of.
> Aye that, O this conscience makes cowardes of vs all,
> Lady in thy orizons, be all my sinnes remembred.

III. The First Quarto, or "bad" Quarto, raises a number of questions.

    A. Is the "bad" Quarto a first draft that Shakespeare later rewrote? Is it a badly printed version of *Hamlet*? Or is it, as some scholars have maintained, a version that was reconstructed by an actor from memory?

    B. The lines given to the character Marcellus in the "bad" Quarto are almost the same in the Second Quarto and the First Folio. One theory is that the actor who played Marcellus reconstructed the play from memory—knowing his own part perfectly but the other parts imperfectly—to earn some extra money.

    C. The bad Quarto seems more akin to everyday speech than the elevated, organized rhetoric of the Second Quarto and the First Folio.

IV. In contrast to the fluid text of *Hamlet*, let's look at a seemingly secure text, Shakespeare's Sonnet 87. The sonnets were published, most likely without the author's permission, in 1609.

    A. In Sonnet 87, Shakespeare uses the vocabulary of commerce to express relationships of love.

    B. Like all of Shakespeare's sonnets, this one is organized into three quatrains, that is, three sets of four lines, and a concluding couplet. The governing figurative language relates to love

> Farewell! thou art too dear for my possessing,
> And like enough thou know'st thy estimate,
> The charter of thy worth gives thee releasing;
> My bonds in thee are all determinate.
> For how do I hold thee but by thy granting?
> And for that riches where is my deserving?
> The cause of this fair gift in me is wanting,
> And so my patent back again is swerving.
> Thy self thou gavest, thy own worth then not knowing,
> Or me to whom thou gav'st it else mistaking;
> So thy great gift, upon misprision growing,
> Comes home again, on better judgement making.
> Thus have I had thee, as a dream doth flatter,
> In sleep a king, but waking no such matter.

and economy. New words, and old words used in new contexts, express the idea of love as a kind of investment.

1. The word *dear* gives us an example of polysemy. It can mean either *beloved* or *costly*. Thus, "thou are too dear for my possessing" might mean that Shakespeare's love is too wonderful for him or too expensive for him.

2. *Charter* and *estimate* are words of the new economy. A *charter*, for example, is a contract. Is love a contractual relationship?

3. The line "My bonds in thee are all determinate" means that the investment of love has matured. In the 16th century, *determine* also meant to understand the terms in which something was written. Thus, polysemy creates a double meaning in every line.

C. Many of the important words in this sonnet use the *mis*-prefix: *mistaking, misprision*. Shakespeare says, in effect, that his love gave herself to him because she didn't know her own worth.

1. *Misprision* means to wrongly value something. The word *prise* in Middle English meant *value* or *reputation*.

2. Chaucer, for example, notes that the knight had a "sovereign price," meaning perhaps both an estimable reputation and a price in sovereigns.

D. This sonnet seems to be about both exchanges and language itself. To read the poem in Shakespeare's time is to be sensitive to the fact that in a polysemous world, all utterances are ambiguous.

E. The line "Thus have I had thee, as a dream doth flatter,/In sleep a king, but waking no such matter" recalls the longstanding association of dreaming and sleep with the imaginative world of poetry. We see here, too, another form of exchange—exchanging oneself in sleep for a role in dreams.

V. What can we learn about pronunciation and spelling in this sonnet?

A. Several rhymes in Sonnet 87 no longer seem to work in Modern English. Consider, for example, *possessing* and *releasing*.

1. These two words probably rhymed on the sound /ɛ/: "possessing" and "relessing."

2. The vowels of these two words had different origins, but for a period of time in the history of English pronunciation, their sounds fell together and enabled Shakespeare to rhyme them.

B. We see another example of two words that no longer rhyme in *granting* and *wanting*.

    1. As mentioned in an earlier lecture, the "w-" sound has a tendency to affect the sound of the vowel following it in everyday speech. A vowel in a position after "w-" is usually rounded: *war, want, was*.

    2. In Shakespeare's time, this tendency to round the vowel had not yet formed, which enabled him to rhyme these two words *granting* and *wanting*.

C. With regard to spelling, two words are of particular interest: *ritches* and *guift* (*riches* and *gift*).

    1. *Ritches* was almost never spelled with a "t," either in French or in English. Linguists would call the insertion of the "t" a case of "articulative intrusion," that is, the habit of intruding into the pronunciation of a word a sound that isn't there because the mouth is in a position to produce certain sounds. A modern example can is the "p-" sound that can sometimes be heard in the pronunciation of *something*.

    2. The spelling of *guift* reflects a convention adopted from French spellings by Renaissance printers to indicate a hard "g-" sound. The "g-" of *gift* was to be pronounced in the same way as in the French *Guillaume* or *guerre*.

VI. In this lecture and the previous one, we've seen both the familiar and the alien in Shakespeare, and we've learned that we should hear not only the great quotations in Shakespeare but also the unquotable features of the language of his time.

Reading:

Paul Bertram and Bernice W. Kliman, eds., *The Three-Text Hamlet*.

Frank Kermode, *Shakespeare's Language*.

Leah Marcus, *Unediting the Renaissance*.

Stephen Orgel and A. R. Braunmiller, *The Pelican Shakespeare*.

George Steiner, *After Babel: Aspects of Language and Translation*.

Questions to Consider:

1. Might Shakespeare be more accessible to some readers if the quarto texts were used?

2. What features of value does the quarto text retain that are missing in the Folio version?

Lecture Nineteen—Transcript
Shakespeare—Poetry, Sound, Sense

"To be or not to be?" That is a question not just for Hamlet, but for us. What is the authentically "Shakespearian"? What is the relationship between what we imagine to be Shakespeare's intention and the way in which that intention showed up on the stage and on the page?

The medium of print during the Renaissance was almost as variable as writing itself. Books were very often proofread in the course of their production. Type fonts would break, individual texts would be corrected or left uncorrected, and the individual printed book could be as unique an object as an individual handwritten manuscript.

When we look at Shakespeare's plays and poems, we are looking at documents of Renaissance book making, and very often, these documents reflect the variations and, if you like, the mutations of the print shop from the sound of stage or the mind of the author.

In the case of *Hamlet*, we have one of the most famous and distinctive of Shakespeare's plays that comes down to us in several versions. There is, of course, the version of the play that appears in the 1623 First Folio, published posthumously. But there are two earlier versions of the play in Quartos. Now, just to pause for a minute, a Folio is a large printed volume and a Quarto is a small printed volume and that's all you really need to know. The Quartos were smaller, if you like, hand-sized or pocket-sized volumes.

The first time *Hamlet* was printed was in 1603, in something we call The First Quarto. The *Hamlet* of 1603 is short, it seems garbled, the language is remarkably different, and much of the structure and idiom of the play is almost unrecognizable.

In 1604, there was another quarto printed. This is the so-called Second Quarto. Here the play is longer, the speeches are more representative of what we know, the disposition of the lines among the actors, the way in which the play is organized, the arc and sweep of the tragedy is far more familiar to us. So modern editions of *Hamlet* are based largely on the texts that appeared in the Second Quarto of 1604, and the First Folio of 1623.

In those texts, what modern editors give us is a great soliloquy. And so, let me begin with this great soliloquy and let's look at it as a specimen of Shakespearian language.

> To be, or not to be: that is the question:
> Whether 'tis nobler in the mind to suffer
> The slings and arrows of outrageous fortune,
> Or to take arms against a sea of troubles,
> And by opposing end them? To die: to sleep;
> No more; and by a sleep to say we end
> The heart-ache and the thousand natural shocks
> That flesh is heir to, 'tis a consummation
> Devoutly to be wish'd. To die, to sleep;
> To sleep: perchance to dream: ay, there's the rub;
> For in that sleep of death what dreams may come
> When we have shuffled off this mortal coil,
> Must give us pause.

I'll pause there. These familiar lines give us the sense and shape of Shakespeare's rhetoric. The question and answer motif, the setup of a problem. Now, in the schoolroom and the university, students would have been educated by posing problems. This is like, if you've done for example, high school debate—resolved, and then you have a resolution. For example, resolved: the internal combustion engine has been a great benefit to human society. Then you had to come up with an argument for and an argument against.

Well, in the medieval, the Renaissance schoolroom, in Shakespeare's time as well, the question might be very general. For example, should a man marry? You would be expected to argue for and against. So the question is the Latin *questio*—that's where our word *question* comes from—but it's not an interrogation, rather it is a topic for debate. What is the *questio* for today, class? To be or not to be. You would be expected to take one side or you'd be expected to take another side.

What Hamlet does in this soliloquy is he takes the *questio* of the schoolroom and he turns it into an inner discussion. He takes both the pro and the con. And so, Hamlet goes on, "To suffer the slings and arrows of outrageous fortune."

And on and on. These are the extended metaphors, the figurative forms, these are the schemae and the tropes that Shakespeare would

©2008 The Teaching Company.

have learned from the rhetorical manuals of his time. So I want to begin with the great soliloquy by showing you that it is generated not simply out of the imagination of the playwright or the despondency of the character, but really out of the assignments of the classroom.

Let's look at the passage in a little more detail. This is a passage that works through repetition. Now, in the rhetorical manuals of the Renaissance, repetition was called "anaphora"—that is, the repeating of an initial word or phrase at the beginning of a line, a sentence or a clause. "To die, to sleep," that is repeated twice. If you know the play or if you hear it as I read it, what you'll know is that "to die, to sleep," appears twice, and when it does appear, it appears in the same place in the line. "And by opposing end them? To die: to sleep;" and then several lines later: "Devoutly to be wish'd. To die, to sleep."

Shakespeare, remember, is writing scanned verse. It's iambic pentameter verse that is unrhymed. He's not just repeating words, but he's repeating them at the same point in the line and his audience, attentive to the sway of syntax and the play of meter, would have heard this. The anaphora here is metrical and it's aural. What you see on the page, what you hear in the ear locates "to die: to sleep," at the same place. "Ay, there's the rub."

Now, "the rub"—what it really means—is it was an obstruction to a bowler's ball in a game. Imagine life as a game of nine pins. Do you strike or do you spare? Ay, there's the rub. We could go on in great detail analyzing this passage, but what I'd like to do is I'd like to turn from, if you like, the good Shakespeare that we want him to be, to the bad Shakespeare that we don't want him to be.

In the First Quarto text of 1603, the soliloquy appears as follows (and I'm going to read the opening lines of it):

> To be, or not to be, I there's the point,
> To Die, to sleepe, is that all? I all:
> No, to sleepe, to dreame, I mary there it goes,
> For in that sleepe of death, when wee awake,
> And borne before an euerlasting Iudge,
> From whence no passenger euer retur'nd,
> The vndiscouered country, at whose sight
> The happy smile, and the accursed damn'd.
> But for this, the ioyfull hope of this,
> Whol'd beare the scornes and flattery of the world,

Scorned by the right rich, the rich curssed of the poore?
The widow being oppressed, the orphan wrong'd,
The taste of hunger, or a tirants raigne,
And a thousand more calamities besides,
To grunt and sweate vnder this weary life,
When that he may his full Quietus make,
With a bare bodkin, who would this indure,
But for a hope of something after death?
Which pusles the braine, and doth confound the sence,
Which makes vs rather beare those euilles we haue,
Than flie to others that we know not of.
I that, O this conscience makes cowardes of vs all,
Lady in thy orizons, be all my sinnes remembred.

I've read this very differently than I read the good version, and I read it because this comes off as something garbled. It comes off as something—how can I put it— improvised; it comes off as something far more colloquial than the good version. That is, in the good version, we can see the precision of anaphora and the precision of balance.

One of the things we can also see in the "good" version is enjambment. "Enjambment" is the technique of having a line run on—that is, where the end of a line is not the end of a sentence. So, in the good version, "To die: to sleep; / No more; and by a sleep to say we end / The heart-ache and the thousand natural shocks / That flesh is heir to." You have to read it as a sentence—each clause doesn't end with a line.

Many people believe that it is the mark of sophisticated poetry not to end each clause with the end of the line, but in the "bad" Quarto edition, just about every single clause and every single sentence ends with a line. So it's a sequence of broken-up lines rather than a flow of sentences.

"That is the question," versus "I, there's the point." Well, it's not a point, it's a question or it's a problem, or it's a decision to be made. "To die, to sleep, is that all?" Now "To die, to sleep, is that all" sort of runs more like a colloquialism than, "To die, to sleep; to sleep: perchance to dream."

"I mary there it goes," this is a far more colloquial version of it than the original. Is this a sleep of death or is it a dream of death? This is

©2008 The Teaching Company.

the wonderful thing, "for in that sleep of death, what dreams may come?" That's the phrase of the "good" version. The "bad" version is, "for in that dream of death, when we awake."

Let me ask you, what do you like better? Is death a dream or is death a sleep? One prompts a version of imaginative association—that is, death and sleep, sleep and poetry—but dreaming and death implies something else. It implies that death is just something that is imagined. "Whips and scorns of time fly to others that we know not of." These are the kinds of phrases that stick in the mind, and these are the phrases from the "good" version.

But in the "bad" version, "To hope of something after death." What we have here feels like something more like paraphrase, it seems to me—something clichéd. In the "bad" Quarto, we have something like, "you can think of lots of things here," and what's going on is a kind of collocation of imagined conditions or responses, rather than a well-thought-out rhetorical pattern.

What's also interesting about the "bad" version is that it uses some phrasings that are really relatively new and new to colloquial English for the late-16th and early-17th centuries. I mentioned "the widow being oppressed." This kind of phrasing here instead of "the oppressor's wrong" and so on and so on, "the widow being oppressed"—it's that use of the new "-ing" form that is characteristic of idiomatic spoken English. So there's something about the "bad" Quarto that feels simply more idiomatic and more spoken than what we have.

What is the "bad" Quarto? What is the difference between the "good" *Hamlet* and the "bad" *Hamlet*? There have been many questions raised as to what this is. We have a version that may be, 1) it may be an early Shakespearian assay. It may be a trying-out. It may be a kind of initial draft that Shakespeare rewrote. 2) It may be something that is a garbled or badly printed or badly remembered version of the "good" *Hamlet*—that is, it may be something that is maybe a printer's error or a problem of transcription or of mis-remembrance. 3) (and what some scholars have thought for a long time) is that what the "bad" Quarto is, is a copy that was memorially reconstructed by an actor.

What's very interesting is that the character of Marcellus in the "bad" Quarto, has lines that seem to be the right lines. In other words, they show up almost the same in the Second Quarto and in the First Folio. So one theory is the actor who was playing Marcellus decided to make a little bit of cash and so he reconstructed the play from memory—knowing his own part perfectly, but other parts imperfectly.

So he put this thing together and what you get is a kind of garbled, if you like, half-assed Shakespeare. Whatever is going on here, my gut feeling, is that what we're hearing in the "bad" Quarto is something more akin to speech—something more colloquial; more like the sound of talk rather than the elevated organization of schoolroom rhetoric that the Second Quarto and the First Folio give us.

Shakespeare good and Shakespeare bad. If I'm trying to disabuse notions of "goodness" and "badness," let's look at an example of what we might think of as an undeniably good version of Shakespeare. I'd like to turn from play to poem. I'd like to look at Shakespeare's Sonnet 87.

Shakespeare's sonnets were published most likely without his permission in an edition in 1609. The printed text of the sonnets—like the texts in other cases, like we saw such as in *Richard III*—the text of the sonnet is also a fascinating document of print history. What I'm going to do is I'm going to read you this sonnet and then I'm going to talk about some of the reasons why some of the words rhyme, some of the key features of the vocabulary, and the way in which this sonnet is an essay, if you like, in the vocabulary of commerce to express relationships of love. In other words, this is as much a story about love and money as, let's say, the play *The Merchant of Venice* is a story about love and money.

Here is Shakespeare's Sonnet 87:

> Farewell! thou art too dear for my possessing,
> And like enough thou know'st thy estimate,
> The charter of thy worth gives thee releasing;
> My bonds in thee are all determinate.
> For how do I hold thee but by thy granting?
> And for that riches where is my deserving?
> The cause of this fair gift in me is wanting,
> And so my patent back again is swerving.
> Thy self thou gavest, thy own worth then not knowing,
> Or me to whom thou gav'st it else mistaking;

So thy great gift, upon misprision growing,
Comes home again, on better judgement making.
Thus have I had thee, as a dream doth flatter,
In sleep a king, but waking no such matter.

Like all of Shakespeare's sonnets, it's organized into three quatrains—three sets of four lines—and then a concluding couplet. What is the governing figurative language here? The vocabulary is a vocabulary about love and economy. It uses old words in new contexts and new words to express love as a kind of investment. As I've suggested, this sonnet is a kind of version of *The Merchant of Venice*, where investments in ships are made waiting for them to come home again. The word *bond* resonates with the language of Shylock: "I will have my bond."

Dear means costly, but it also means *beloved*. Here, at the beginning of the 17th century, you have an example of polysemy. "Farewell, you are too dear for my possessing," can mean you're just too beloved—you're too wonderful for me. What it can also mean is you're too expensive for me to keep as a girlfriend—you're too dear for my possessing—you're running up a bill.

Charter; *estimate*; these are the words of the new economy. You know your estimate, you know what you're worth. "The charter of thy worth gives thee releasing." Magna Carta, charta. Charta or Carta just means a big piece of paper. So the charter is a contract between two people. Is love a contractual relationship? "My bonds in thee are all determinate." What that means is that I have invested in you as one purchases a bond, and they have come to term—that is, the investment that I've made in you is maturing—determinate. But to determine, in the 16th century, means also to understand the terms in which something has been written. So polysemy—the levels of language and vocabulary here—are creating, if you like, a double meaning in every line.

This sonnet is also a sonnet full of mistakes—that is, many of the important words use the "mis-" prefix at the beginning, so you have *mistaking* and *misprision*. What the sonneteer says is, in effect, you gave yourself to me because you didn't know your own worth, or you didn't know my worth to whom you had given yourself because you mistook it, and so your great gift is growing on misprision.

Misprison doesn't mean prison. It doesn't mean to imprison wrongly, it means to mis-value. To prise (P-R-I-S-E), is to put a price on. The word *price* (pronounced "preece")—*price* in Middle English—means *value* or *reputation*. Chaucer can use it potentially in two ways. When in his description of the knight in the General Prologue of the *Canterbury Tales*, he says that everywhere the knight went, he had a sovereign *preece*—that is, he had an estimable or sovereign value or reputation. But it can also mean, I think, that the knight had a price in sovereigns. In other words, that he was a mercenary; that he had a price in coins with the sovereign's picture on them—that's why we call them *sovereigns*.

What we have here is a sense, again, of polysemy—to value or to misvalue. "My patent back again is swerving." *Patent* doesn't mean rights on an invention—that is a meaning that does not appear until the 19th century. *Patent* means a form of release—that is, I've yielded my patent up to him. That's a kind of phrase which suggests that the commercial vocabulary again is being invoked here. This is a poem about exchanges, but it's also a poem about language itself, in other words, if so many of these words have double meanings.

To learn to read the poem in Shakespeare's own time is to be acutely sensitive to the fact that in a polysemous world, all utterances are ambiguous. It is a poem not just about exchange between lovers, it is a poem about exchange in language. What does it mean to exchange one thing for another?

> Thus have I had thee, as a dream doth flatter,
> In sleep a king, but waking no such matter.

> [My relationship to you has been like a dream, and such a dream flatters me. In my sleep, I am a king, but when I wake, I am nothing like a king at all. I'm just me.]

Go back now to the image of sleep and dream and death in *Hamlet*, because the notion of dream and sleep on the one hand, and of the imaginative world of poetry, is one of the great sustaining associations throughout the Western literary tradition.

John Keats in the early 19th century can write a poem called "Sleep and Poetry." So the relationship between sleeping and dreaming, death and the imagination, place us here again in the world of exchange. I exchange myself for a role: in sleep, a king. Go back to

Henry IV, Part I, from my earlier lecture. "Stand you now for my father?"

Prince Hal says to Falstaff, "You now, play the king or you play me and I will play the king." "To play the king" is central to the theme of *Hamlet*, and playing the king is central to all of Shakespeare's poetry—in sleep, I play the king.

These are the larger metaphors. This is the arc of imaginative language that's at work in this sonnet, but I want to say a few things about pronunciation. There are several rhymes in this sonnet that no longer seem to work in modern English. The sound of the sonnet helps us understand how certain words were pronounced and it tells us something about the history of pronunciation more generally at this time. For example, Shakespeare rhymes the words *possessing* and *releasing*. It's very clear that these words are supposed to rhyme. How do they rhyme?

I'm going to get technical here, but I want to explain it in some detail. These probably rhymed on the sound /ɛ/—that is, "possaissing" and "relaising." Now the word "relaise" comes from a Middle English combination which would have been pronounced "eh." "Possaissing" has a shorter sound—that is, "euh." "Ehh," and "euh." During the course of the Great Vowel Shift, these sounds, for a period of time, actually merged. One of the things that's also changing, you'll remember, is that vowel length—that is, the period of time you hold a vowel—is also no longer a phonemic quality in English. In other words, it just doesn't matter; it doesn't contribute to meaning.

You have issues of vowel quality and you have issues of vowel quantity. The historical explanation is to say that two words with two vowels of different origin, for a particular period of time in the history of English pronunciation, fall together, and Shakespeare can rhyme on them: "possaissing" and "relaising."

There is another rhyme here which I think also needs to be explained and that is the rhyme on *granting* and *wanting*. You'll remember from my previous lecture where I talked about issues of pronunciation in the passage from *Richard III*, that the "w-"—the glide—has a tendency to affect the vowel following it in everyday speech. In Modern spoken English, we tend to round our vowels after a "w-"—that is, we say the "w-" and our lips are remaining in the rounded position—"wuh"—so that the vowel after the "w" is going to be changed. *Car*, but "woar;" *can't*, but "wahnt;" *has*, but "wuz."

This was not always so. There was a time when you could actually rhyme irrespective of the "w." So what I would suggest is that what Shakespeare is doing is he's rhyming *granting* and *wanting*—that is, it is an "e" sound: "*grenting*" and "*wenting*," where the "w's" rounding has not affected permanently the standard pronunciation of English.

Let me say something about spelling. I present this text in its old spelling—that is, in the forms of spelling in the 1609 edition. Two words in particular are interesting: *riches* and *gift*. Now *riches* is spelled R-I-T-C-H-E-S. We almost never spelled it that way. It never was spelled that way in French and it was rarely, if ever, spelled that way in English.

This is what linguists would call a case of "articulative intrusion"—that is, articulative intrusion is the habit of intruding in the pronunciation of a word a sound that isn't there, because the mouth is in a position to produce certain kinds of sounds. For example, a very good example of articulative intrusion is the way that some people pronounce the word *something*. If you say *something* very quickly, your lips are in the position of the "m" and then they're about to go in the position of the "th"—"*something*." Some people will pronounce "*something*" as if there's a "p" in it: "somep-thing." There's no "p" in *something*, but the "p" sound is articulatively intruded in the course of saying it—"something."

When you say *riches*, there is a time when, depending on how you say it, you may intrude the "t" sound—"ritches." Your tongue is at the alveolar ridge, and in spoken English "t" is an alveolar sound: "t," "ritches." So what the printer has done is he has inserted the "t" to indicate the pronunciation.

By contrast, the printer has spelled *gift* G-U-I-F-T. The printer here wants to indicate that "guh" is a hard sound. It's not "jift," but it's *gift*. This is a spelling convention that Renaissance printers adopted from French spellings, where the G-U spelling was used to indicate the "guh" sound. So that, for example in G-E-N-R-E, you'd say "jenre." You wouldn't say "guenre," but if you wanted a "guh" sound, like *Guillaume*, or *guerre*, you'd spell it "gu-." So here is another spelling convention that's designed to indicate a certain kind of pronunciation. These are details that make Shakespeare's familiar language strange. It creates in our minds a sense of the historical distance between ourselves and Shakespeare.

In this lecture and in the previous one, what I've tried to do is I've tried to show you both the familiar and the alien. Just when we think we know what's going on, we encounter a sound, a spelling, an idiom, a text, a version that makes us move towards the exotic. We should not only hear the great quotations in Shakespeare but we should hear the unquotable things as well. Things in Shakespeare are not only magnificent and beautiful but they reflect the nature of the language in its time, its changes and its transformations, the sounds of his speech, the foibles and the fissures on the stage and the fractures of the letters on the page.

Lecture Twenty
The Bible in English

Scope:

From the time of King Alfred on, the Bible was translated into English. Each period of the English language produced its own distinctive versions of the Bible, and the study of these translations can tell us much about the history of the language and the ways in which biblical translation helped to shape the forms of speech.

In this lecture, we will explore the history of biblical translation by examining closely Matthew 17:13–15 from four representative texts: the Old English version from the Late West Saxon period (10th century); the translation made under the supervision of John Wycliffe in the 1380s; the translation published by William Tyndale in 1526; and the King James version, prepared by a group of scholars under the commission of James I of England and published in 1611. The first three translations are based on the Latin Vulgate. The King James translators used other sources, including the Hebrew of the Old Testament and the Greek of the New Testament, but they also incorporated many phrases from earlier English translations, especially that of Tyndale.

Outline

I. Next to Shakespeare, the King James Bible, printed in 1611, was perhaps the most important influence on subsequent speakers, readers, and writers of English.

   A. In this lecture, we'll look at the history of Bible translation, attending to four areas of difference: vocabulary, syntax and grammar, pronunciation, and style.

   B. The passage we'll explore is Matthew 17:13–15, which illustrates some of the changes we're concerned with most pointedly. We begin with the version from the King James Bible.

   C. One of the main features that marks this passage as "biblical" is its paratactic structure—a structure of repeated sentences or clauses joined together by conjunctions. This structure is characteristic of biblical narrative from its origins and was continued by the translators of the King James Bible.

> 13 Then the disciples understood that he spake unto them of John the Baptist.
>
> 14 And when they were come to the multitude, there came to him a certain man, kneeling down to him, and saying:
>
> 15 Lord, have mercy on my son: for he is lunatick, and sore vexed: for ofttimes he falleth into the fire, and oft into the water.

D. The King James Bible also brings together a history of Bible translation. The translators were charged with going back to original texts in Greek, Hebrew, Syrian, Latin, and Aramaic and with reviewing earlier translations of the Bible.

E. We can note, in the King James version, a difference between Old English or native vocabulary and Latinate, French, or Romance vocabulary.

II. The Bible was translated into Old English at various times during the Anglo-Saxon period. We see our text in a West Saxon version, probably from the early 11th century.

> 13 Þa on geton hys leorningcnihtas þæt he hyt sæde be Iohanne am fulluhtere
>
> 14 And þa he com to þære menegu, him to genealæhte sum mann, gebig edum cneowum toforan him and cwæð,
>
> 15 Drihten, gemiltsa minum suna, for þam þe he ys fylle seoc, and yfel þolade; oft he fylð on fyr, and gelomlice on wæter.

A. One of the first things we notice about this passage is that the word *disciples*, which will be the word used throughout later biblical translation, is *leorningcnihtas* ("knights of learning"). This is one of those magnificent Old English noun compounds known as kennings.

B. In this passage, *John the Baptist* is *Iohanne am fulluhtere*, the latter word meaning *to put fully under water*. *Multitude* is *menegu* (*the many*) and the phrase *on bended knees* is *gebig* *edum cneowum*. These examples remind us that Old English was a profoundly inflected language; meaning was determined not by word order but by case endings.

C. In such terms as *Drihten* (*Lord*) and *fylle seoc* (*falling sick*), we can see the common core of Old English vocabulary used to describe experience and translate Scripture.

D. The verb *to suffer* in Old English is *tholian*. Seamus Heaney in his recent translation of *Beowulf* remembers this as a dialect word of the English spoken in Northern Ireland during his childhood. The word also appears in an episode of *Star Trek*, in which the Enterprise is attacked by an evil empire of Tholians.

E. Again, word order was not the primary bearer of meaning in Old English, but word order was regularized to signal temporal or conditional clauses. In Old English, such clauses were signaled not by *when* and *then* but by *þa* or *ðone*.

    1. The two words in Old English could mean either *then* or *when*. The only way to signal meaning was through the word order pattern that followed the word.

    2. When *þa* or *ðone* was followed by a verb, then the subject, the meaning was "then": *Þa on geton hys leorningcnihtas.* (*Then understood the knights of learning.*)

    3. When either word was followed by the subject, then the verb, the meaning was *when*: *And þa he com to þære menegu* (*And when they came to the multitude*).

III. Our Middle English text is a translation prepared by the disciples of John Wycliffe. In the late 14th century, Wycliffe founded the heretical movement known as Lollardy, which some historians have seen as a proto-Protestant reform movement. Central to Lollardy was the idea that the reading and experience of the Scriptures should be in the vernacular.

A. With this version, we immediately see Latin and French loan words used in place of native Old English coinages: *disciples*, *company*, *mercy*, *people*, *lunatic*, *suffer*.

B. *Lunatic*, meaning *under the domination of the moon*, replaces *falling sick* in the Old English version. To be *lunatic* was to be subject to the variable phases of the moon. Note that Wycliffe not only enhances the vocabulary of biblical English, but he also provides a model for later translators.

> 13 Thanne disciplis vndurstoden, that of Joon Baptist he hadde seide to hem.
>
> 14 And whanne he cam to the cumpanye of peple, a man cam to hym folded on knees byfor hym, seying, Lord, haue mercy on my sone; for he is lunatyke, and suffrith yuel, for why oft tymys he fallith in to the fijr, and oft tymys in to the water.

IV. The next major figure to offer a Bible in English was William Tyndale, working in the 1520s. During this period, just before the English Reformation under King Henry VIII, it was against the law to write and publish a Bible in English. Thus, Tyndale's version of the New Testament was published in Geneva.

    A. Here, we note several differences in vocabulary. Tyndale retains the word *disciple*, for example, but he replaces *understood* with *perceaved*. *Understand* is, essentially, an Anglo-Saxonism, but Tyndale prefers the more complex, Latinate *perceive*. He may have been placing an emphasis on the interiority of the disciples.

> 13 Then his disciples perceaved, that he spake vnto them of Jhon baptist.
>
> 14 And when they were come to the people, ther cam to hym a certayne man, and kneled doune to hym, saying:
>
> 15 Master, have mercy on my sonne; ffor he is franticke, and ys sore vexed, and oft tymes falleth into the fyre, and oft into the water.

    B. The switch from *lunatic* to *frantic* and from *suffereth evil* to *sore vexed* gives the text a feeling of heightened, portentous rhetoric. Tyndale is not simply translating the Bible but creating a biblical idiom in English. Such phrases as *spake unto them* or *were come to the people* foster the impression of something memorable and important.

C. In the latter phrase, the use of the verb *to be* rather than *to have* as the modal verb, or helping verb, may be a conscious archaism. Old Germanic and Old English grammar used forms of the verb *to be* to indicate a change of state, and Tyndale seems to call on these forms for special effect in his translation.

D. We can see something of the sound of Tyndale in his spellings. For example, the spelling of *perceaved* signals a contemporary pronunciation. But the spelling of *saying* maintains an older convention from Chancery English.

E. We might characterize the style of Tyndale as "Bible-talk"—a familiar blend of the colloquial and the archaic. Many of Tyndale's idioms and phrasings were adapted by the King James translators nearly a century later. Thus, when we look at the King James, we see not simply a translation from original scriptural texts but a translation that is conscious of the history of English Bible translation.

V. The King James Bible is not a translation into the everyday speech or written communication of 1611 but a deliberately archaic form of the language that maintains distinctive syntactic and verbal features that can be traced back to earlier translations.

A. In some cases, the King James translators rejected Tyndale's phrasings in favor of earlier ones; Tyndale's *perceived*, for example, is returned to Wycliffe's *understood*. In other cases, Tyndale-isms are retained: "spake *unto* them," "when they *were come*." Many of these choices were probably made for poetic effect.

B. Even for readers of the King James Bible in its own time, *falleth* and *doest* would have been perceived as archaic or heightened grammatical forms.

C. It's interesting to note that whether the Bible is written in English or any other European language, God is addressed informally. But in using the form *thou*, which was probably just on the cusp of archaism at the time this Bible was produced, the King James may have contributed to the illusion that *thou* and *thee* are formal or heightened forms.

D. These forms of the King James Bible would have a great impact on English and American writing throughout the 18th,

19th, and 20th centuries. Such writers as Walt Whitman, Abraham Lincoln, Herman Melville, Mark Twain, and Joel Chandler Harris will evoke the sounds of the King James and bits and pieces of biblicism to create a narrative form.

E. Both Shakespeare and the King James Bible not only look back to earlier grammatical forms and pronunciations, but they also look ahead to the kind of impact they will have on the English language in the future. As we leave the world of Shakespeare and King James, we enter the beginnings of Modern English.

Reading:

W. F. Bolton, *A Living Language: The History and Structure of English* (from which material in this lecture is adapted).

David Lawton, "Englishing the Bible," in David Wallace, ed., *The Cambridge History of Medieval English Literature*.

Questions to Consider:

1. How does the vocabulary of various biblical translations into English change over time?

2. In what ways is the King James Bible superior—or inferior—to the more recent Revised Standard Version?

Lecture Twenty—Transcript
The Bible in English

Shakespeare, as we have seen and heard, bequeathed to modern speakers, readers, and writers of English a range of vocabulary and a vividness of syntax, imagination, and figurative expression. But Shakespeare was, of course, not the only, nor even perhaps the only major, influence from Renaissance England on subsequent forms of English.

The King James Bible—that product of royal commission; that product of group translation, that saw print in 1611—the King James Bible was, next to Shakespeare, perhaps the most important influence on subsequent speakers, readers, and writers of English.

In this lecture, I want to look at the history of Bible translation. I want to look not only at the King James therefore, but at the range of "English-ings" of the Bible to see how, in so many ways, the history of English is a history of Bible translation.

As we saw in Shakespeare, and as we saw in so many other texts I've looked at, we're going to attend to four areas of difference in our study of biblical translation. We're going to look at vocabulary, syntax and grammar, pronunciation (or sound), and style. Now the passage that I've chosen is a nice one. It's a short passage from the book of Matthew in the New Testament, Mathew 17:13–15. It's a good passage because it illustrates some of these changes most pointedly. It's a good passage because New Testament translation is something that is sustained more vividly and more pointedly than Old Testament translation from the Old English through the Modern English period, and also because there are some nice little vocabulary terms in here that can help us review some of the key themes and structures of the course.

Let me read to you the passage first in the King James Bible version. Here we have Matthew 17:13–15:

13 Then the disciples understood that he spake unto them of John the Baptist.

14 And when they were come to the multitude, there came to him a certain man, kneeling down to him, and saying,

15 Lord, have mercy on my son: for he is lunatick, and sore
    vexed: for ofttimes he falleth into the fire, and oft into
    the water.

This passage gives us the full flavor of, if you like, King James English. What is "biblical" about it? What is "biblical" about it first of all is what we might call paratactic structure. Paratactic structure means a structure of repeated sentences or clauses joined together by conjunctions, such as *and*—and then this happened, and then that happened, and then that happened. This kind of paratactic structure is characteristic of biblical narrative—it's not something that is invented by King James for it's characteristic of the Bible's narrative going back to its origins—but the King James translators bring it out in especially particular ways.

Also what the King James Bible does is it brings together a history of Bible translation—that is, the King James translators were not simply going back to original texts in Greek, in Hebrew, in Syriac, in Latin, and in Aramaic—the King James Bible translators were also charged with reviewing the history of Bible translation. In the course of this lecture, what you will see and hear are the ways in which earlier translations of the Bible into English make it into *King James*.

What you also, I hope, heard in the passages I read you just now, and that at this point in the course, I hope that you are sensitive to, is a difference between the Old English or native vocabulary on the one hand, and the Latinate, or French, or Romance vocabulary on the other. So you can see and hear words like *disciples, multitude, certain, mercy, lunatic*. These are words that come from a French or Latin vocabulary, and they are opposed to words from the native English vocabulary.

We're going to see, in the course of this lecture, how this vocabulary structure operates.

Let's begin, then, at the beginning. The English Bible was rendered into Old English during a set of moments in the Anglo-Saxon intellectual life. We saw early on how Bede represented the Northumbrian efflorescence; how King Alfred represented the rise of scholarship at Wessex; and how Aethelwold, Bishop of Winchester after Alfred, represented the so-called Benedictine revival.

What sorted itself out by the 10th and 11th centuries in the Anglo-Saxon world was a version of certain portions of the holy scriptures that were either interlinearly translated—that is, where individuals would write English words over the Latin words of their Bible—or, were written out through. What we have from this Anglo-Saxon period is a version of the Bible in West Saxon. This is probably from the early 11th century.

Here in Old English is the very passage that I just read to you from the King James:

> 13. þa on geton hys leorningcnihtas, þæt he hyt sæde be Ioanne am fulluhtere
>
> 14. And þa he com to þære menegu, him to genealæhte sum mann, gebig edum cneowum toforan him and cwæð:
>
> 15. Drihten, gemiltsa minum suna, for þam þe he ys fylle seoc, and yfel þolade; oft he fylð on fyr, and gelomlice on wæter.

What's the first thing that we notice about this passage? The first thing that we notice about this passage is that the word *disciples*, which is going to be the word throughout the later biblical translation, is *leorningcnihtas* (*knights of learning*). If you were a master of learning, you were a teacher. If you were a knight of learning, you are a student or a disciple. *Leorningcnihtas* is one of those magnificent Old English noun compounds that we saw in the poetry of the Anglo-Saxons. It is a kenning, it is a noun metaphor.

You will remember how Old English poetry from Caedmon on coined its words rather than borrowed them. What we have here is *leorningcnihtas*, if you like, a word that comes out of that metaphorical vocabulary to express someone who is a disciple—a knight of learning.

John the Baptist is *Ioanne am fulluhtere, fulluhtere* (*to put fully under water*)—that is, he's not John the Baptist, he's John the complete "wetterer," if you like—the one who would fully place you under the water. Multitude is *menegu* (*the many*). We can go through word by word here. On *gebig edum cneowum* (*on bended knees*). The "-um" endings signal here the masculine plural datives. What matters is not that you know this in detail, what matters is that you recognize that this is a profoundly inflected language, and that, as in all Old

©2008 The Teaching Company.

English texts, meaning is determined not primarily by word order, but it is determined by the case endings. *Drihten, Lord.*

Remember in "Caedmon's Hymn," how *Drihten* is one of the words for the Almighty, and remember that it was a word that came from temporal, political landscapes—that is, the *drihten* was the lord of a particular area; he was a temporal or political ruler. It's a word now that is applied to God. *Gemiltsa minum suna* (*Be mild unto my son.*)—*Gemiltsa*, (*be mild*). Why? Because he is *fylle seoc*, (*he is falling sick*). Perhaps this is a medical condition, perhaps this is the Old English way of talking about epilepsy, or the way of talking about madness. We can see like *leorningcnihtas* that this is another word that is made up of compounds, and we can see here the way in which the Old English vocabulary is describing experience and translating scripture based on the common core of the old vocabulary.

Finally, I want to call attention to one word here—one of my favorite words in all Old English— and that is the verb *to suffer*: *þolian*. *Þolian* is the Old English verb *to suffer*—and he suffers. We're told that he *þolade*. *Þolian* is one of these magnificent words that has completely fallen out of the language. Those of you that know Seamus Heaney's great recent translation of *Beowulf*, will know that Heaney spends a great deal of time calling attention to *þolian* as well, because he remembers it as a dialect word of the English spoken in Northern Ireland of his childhood—to *thole* was to suffer.

Those of you that are familiar with the great repertory of American popular culture, *Star Trek* the original series, will remember that great moment when the Enterprise is enmeshed by the Tholeans— that evil alien empire who weave a Tholean web around the ship. Surely some writer for this series must have studied Old English in college and as a little side joke to the philologists in the audience, gives us a moment of suffering as Tholean. *Tholian*—a word that I would advocate returning to the language.

I've spend a good deal of time talking about vocabulary, but I want to say something about the word order in this Old English passage. Word order, you'll remember, is not the primary bearer of meaning in Old English, but there are times when word order needs to be regularized in order to bear that meaning, and here is the case: Old English signaled temporal or conditional clauses, not by using the words *when* and *then*, but by using the word (*þa*) or the word (*ðone*). These are words that can mean *then*, but they could also mean *when*. So *þa* ("tha") and *ðone* ("thona") could mean *then* or *when*.

How do you know the difference? The way you know the difference is by changing the word order pattern that follows it. When you have *þa* or *ðone* followed by the verb, then followed by the subject, it means *then*. So in the Old English, *þa on geton hys leorningcnihtas—then understood* (*on geton*—they *on got*, they got it, they brought in, then got the learning knights); *then the disciples understood*.

But because you only have one word, you have to keep the word order pattern regularized. So *þa* ("tha") followed by a verb, followed by the subject is *then*; *þa* followed by the subject, followed by the verb, means *when*. So in the next sentence, it begins, *And þa he com to þære menegu* (*And when they came to the multitude*).

I want you to get this: *þa he com* is *when they came*: *þa on geton hys leorningcnihtas, then got* (*or understood*) *the knights of learning.*

This is a feature of Old English and it is the one piece of word order patterning that I think is really worth knowing—that is, when you have a limited lexicon, when you have one word that's designed to do two different grammatical things, you need to signal that grammatical difference with word order patterns.

English, from the Middle English period on, has two words, *when* and *then*, and we're going to see this in the Middle English translation of this same passage. This translation was prepared by the disciples of John Wycliffe. John Wycliffe was an ecclesiastical reformer and dissenter in the last decades of the 14th century. He was the founder of the heretical movement known as Lollardy. Some historians have seen Lollardy as a kind of proto-Protestant reform movement. It had many tenets, but one of its central ones was that the reading and experience of the Scriptures should go on in the vernacular—that is, people should be able to read the Bible in their own language. This was heretical at the time.

Here is the Wycliffe-ite, if you like, Middle English translation of the scriptures from the 1380s. It's the vernacular Bible of the time of Chaucer.

13   Thanne disciplis vndurstoden, that of Joon Baptist he hadde seide to hem.

14   And whanne he cam to the cumpanye of peple, a man cam to hym folded oun knees byfor hym, seying, Lord, haue mercy on my sone; for he is lunatyke, and suffrith yuel, for why oft tymes as he fallith in to the fijr, and oft tymes in to the water.

Right away you can tell that there is a difference in vocabulary register—that you have words coming from a learned vocabulary of Latin and French. You have *disciples, company, mercy, people, lunatic,* and *suffer.* This is not *gemiltsa minum suna.* This is not *be mild to my son,* it is *have mercy on my son.* It is a high-concept French word, and he is not simply *falling sick,* but he is *lunatic*—that is, he is under the domination of the moon.

You will remember how Caxton, in 1490, talked about how we English live under the domination of the moon. We're constantly variable. To be lunatic was to be subject to the variable phases of the moon. It's important to note here that Wycliffe is not only enhancing the vocabulary of biblical English. What he's also doing is he's providing a model for later translators.

The next major figure to offer a Bible in English is William Tyndale who is working in the 1520s. During this period of time, just before the English Reformation under King Henry VIII, it is still against the law to write and publish a Bible in English. So Tyndale had to do his work and had to have his Bible published in Geneva. In 1526, his New Testament was published in Geneva. This is Tyndale's version of that passage:

13   Then his disciples perceaved that he spak vnto them of Jhon baptist.

14   And when they were come to the people, ther cam to hym a certayne man, and kneled doune to him, saying:

15   Master, have mercy on my sonne, ffor he is franticke, and ys sore vexed, and oft tymes falleth into the fyre, and oft tymes into the water.

Look at the difference in vocabulary. Tyndale keeps the word *disciple*—which is in the Latin and which Wycliffe adopts—but he doesn't say *understood*, he says *perceived*. Now *understand* is an Englishism; it is an Anglo-Saxonism. Even though the Anglo-Saxon word is *ongetton*, *understand* is made up of *under-stand*. What he does here is he gives us a more complex Latinate term *perceived*. I think that what he's trying to do is he's trying to make this moment a moment of perception rather than a moment of understanding. In other words, the idea is that he is almost psychologizing the response of the disciples—that he's interested, if you like, in the interiority of the disciples.

A fair amount of Tyndale's translation is fascinated with the way in which individuals act out of motive and out of experience. Look also at some of the differences. *Lunatic* becomes *frantic*. This seems more familiar to us but it's not going to be the word that comes into King James. *Lunatic* versus *frantic* and *suffereth evil*: *sore vexed*. What is the feel of Tyndale here?

The feel of Tyndale, it seems to me, is the feel of heightened, almost portentious rhetoric. That is, what I think is going on is not simply a matter of adding or subtracting vocabulary; what is going on is that phrases like *sore vexed*, or words like *master*, or *perceived*, or *frantic*—these are words that are coming from both an old vocabulary and a new vocabulary to create something that Tyndale wants to be memorable. That is, he wants his language to be something truly biblical—that the issue is not simply translating the Bible; the issue is creating a biblical idiom in English.

That really, it seems to me, is Tyndale's accomplishment. So when we look in detail at Tyndale and we compare him to what came before and what came after, you can see that there are certain kinds of forms that become, to put it casually, Bible-talk: *Spake unto them*. When *he spake unto to them*, it's not just that he spoke to them, he spoke *unto* them. There is this need to, if you like, enhance the number of syllables, to make it scan—to create the impression that this is something important: Were come to the people. Not just that they came to the people.

This is, I believe, a conscious archaism—that is, the use of the verb *to be*, rather than the verb *to have*, as your modal or helping verb in showing us how the action is going on. There is an old Germanic tendency in Germanic grammar to use forms of the verb *to be* when you indicate change of state. This shows up in Old English and I think Tyndale is looking back to this kind of conscious archaism to give a heightened feel.

We can see something of the sound of Tyndale, too, in the spellings: his *perceived* (*perceaved*) is spelled P-E-R-C-E-A-V-E-D, "per-say-ved," but he's writing *saying*, S-A-Y. I believe that these spellings are also, much like his vocabulary, is synthesis. On the one hand, he's using certain spellings to indicate pronunciation; on the other hand, he's using certain spellings to, as it were, maintain older Chancery traditions of conventional spellings. So how do you use the spelling of your Bible to indicate pronunciation, or to indicate regularization?

The style of Tyndale, as I'm suggesting, is something that we've come to recognize as Bible-talk—a familiar blend of the colloquial and the archaic. It seems archaic to us because many of its idioms and phrasings were adapted by the King James translators nearly a century later. So when we get to King James, as I suggested, what we're looking at is we're looking at not simply a translation from original scriptural texts, we're looking at a translation that is conscious of, and that absorbs the history of English Bible translation again.

Now let me read the King James passage again:

13 Then the disciples understood that he spake unto them of John the Baptist.

14 And when they were come to the multitude, there came to him a certain man, kneeling down to him, and saying,

15 "Lord, have mercy on my son: for he is lunatick, and sore vexed: for ofttimes he falleth into the fire, and oft into the water."

When we are reading the language of the King James Bible; we are not, I believe, reading the language of everyday speech of 1611, nor are we even reading the language of everyday commerce or of written communication. We are reading a heightened language—a deliberately archaic form that maintains distinctive syntactic and verbal features. And many of these, in fact, do go back to earlier forms.

What the King James translators do is they reject Tyndale's *perceaved* and they leapfrog over Tyndale to Wycliffe's *understood*—that he spoke to them of John the Baptist, he spoke *unto* them. That's Tyndale-talk. When *they were come to*, that's Tyndale-talk, but not when they were come to the *people*, when they were come to the *multitude*. "And when they were come to the multitude." I believe that one of the reasons for choosing a word like *multitude* is its polysyllabic rhythm—that is, it makes the line scan almost poetically different than, "and when they were come to the people"—"And when they were come to the multitude, there came to him a certain man kneeling down to him and saying, 'Lord, have mercy on my son, for he is lunatick.'"

We go back to *lunatic* now, and I believe that in this choice of *lunatic*, the King James Bible reinforces the modern sense of that word, as not simply under the influence of the moon, but rather crazy—*and sore vexed*—but that's a Tyndale-ism. "For ofttimes he falleth into the fire and oft into the water."

We know from a fair amount of historical evidence that people in the 17th century were no longer saying *falleth*, but they were saying *falls*; that they were no longer saying *doest*, but they were saying *do*. "Thou doest, he falleth"—these are grammatical endings to indicate the second person and the third person, respectively. These are phrasings that are conscious archaisms and I believe that for a reader of the King James Bible in its own time, they would have been perceived as archaic or heightened grammatical forms.

Is come again—that Tyndale-ism there. So what we're seeing in King James, as I'm suggesting, is this synthesis. God is addressed informally. Throughout the Bible, whether in English or in any other European language, we pray to God in the informal. "*Der Du von dem Himmel bist.*" That is a German line from Goethe. It is my understanding that many Europeans, when they pray to God, and in the language of the Bibles in the other European languages, address God using the equivalent of the second-person informal.

One prays to God not as a friend, but as an intimate, and God is addressed not as a peer, but as someone, if you like, in the family. What has happened is that the King James Bible—by maintaining this distinction, which may be just on the cusp of archaism at this time—the King James Bible shows us *thou* as a marked or unusual form rather than *you*. It is this form of the use of *thou*, together with the later 17th- and 18th-century Quaker use of *thou* and *thee*—in other words, to signal that we are all brothers or friends—it is this set of uses of *thou* and *thee* that have created the illusion that *thou* and *thee* forms are formal or heightened forms. Grammatically, they are not.

What I want to stress here is that when you read the King James Bible you recognize that it is using the grammatical resources not only of its own time but of the recent past, and that being published in 1611, it's standing on the cusp of language change.

These forms of the King James Bible will have a great impact on English and American writing throughout the 18th, 19th, and 20th centuries. Writers such as Whitman, Lincoln, Melville, Twain, and Joel Chandler Harris in his "Uncle Remus" stories, will evoke the sounds, if you like, of King James and the bits and pieces of Biblicism to create a narrative form.

What I want to suggest in closing here is that Shakespeare and the King James Bible not only look back to earlier grammatical forms and pronunciations, they look ahead to the kind of impact they'll have on the English language in the British Isles and in America and elsewhere. Stories such as the one that I gave you from the New Testament, even the little snippet that I gave you, shows you something also about narrative. It shows you about the ways in which narrative can work through parataxis and through repetition. And it shows you, too, the way in which vocabulary can be uniquely associated with a certain form of heightened Biblicism.

When we leave the world of Shakespeare and we leave the world of the King James Bible, we are entering what is for all intents and purposes, Modern English and the beginnings of our language, not just in England, but in America and beyond.

Lecture Twenty-One
Samuel Johnson and His *Dictionary*

Scope:

In this and the following lecture, we examine the rise of lexicography in the 17th and 18th centuries, with a special focus on the great *Dictionary* of Samuel Johnson (1755). This dictionary stands as the culmination of nearly a century of responses to the growth and change in the English vocabulary. But it also has great impact on all subsequent English and American dictionaries, setting the principles of historical citation, literary quotation, and definitional hierarchy that will be used later in such influential works as the *Oxford English Dictionary* and *Webster's American Dictionary*.

The central question raised in these two lectures is whether the study of language should be prescriptive or descriptive: Should it be designed to look at how we speak and write, then offer guidelines for that practice, or should it simply describe, as best as possible, habits of speech and writing, and leave it at that? More subtly, the question really is, as we will see, whether there is any difference between the two—is any act of description in an official or institutionally sanctioned area (a dictionary, a grammar book, a primer) in itself an act of prescription, simply by virtue of its authority?

Outline

I. In previous lectures, we've seen the remarkable rise in the vocabulary of English in the period from 1500 to 1700, as well as a change in attitude of English speakers to become voracious in their appetite for new words. In this lecture and the following one, we'll explore the ways in which scholars, critics, readers, and writers responded to this increase by developing tools, guides, or interpretive matrices for that vocabulary.

II. The earliest dictionaries in English were lists of what were called "hard words," that is, guides to the new vocabulary of science, trade, and exploration.

    A. John Bullokar published his *Expositor* in 1616, listing words from "logic, law, physics and astronomy."

B. In 1623, Cockeram's *Dictionarie* included definitions for "hard words" in numerous areas.

C. Phillips's *New World of Words* (1658) lists on its title page 41 arts and sciences from which its words were taken. The title of this work seems to be the lexicographical equivalent of the great journeys of exploration and colonization taking place at this time.

D. A characteristic of these early dictionaries was an attention to the details of technology. In 1736, Nathaniel Bailey published his *Dictionary* of "hard and technical words, or terms of art" taken from 62 listed "arts, sciences, and mysteries."

    1. Bailey set out to organize his definitions in hierarchical form.

    2. He was interested in etymology and in the relationship between figurative and literal expression. One question that emerged for lexicographers in the 18th century was whether one should privilege the figurative meaning over the literal meaning, even if the literal meaning has passed out of use.

III. Samuel Johnson (1709–1784) was a lexicographer, literary critic, poet, essayist, and tastemaker to his generation.

    A. In addition to his famous work on the *Dictionary*, Johnson wrote a variety of critical, interpretive, and poetic works that give voice to his psychological and aesthetic vision of the world.

        1. Johnson was preoccupied with notions of transitoriness and mutability. One of his poems was titled "The Vanity of Human Wishes," and one of his works of prose fiction, *Rasselas*, was keyed to the idea of the mutable and the vain.

        2. Johnson was also concerned with the question of whether or not particular works of literature and particular texts in the English language would have an afterlife.

    B. For Johnson, the idea of the *Dictionary* began in the 1740s. He found a patron for the work in Lord Chesterfield and, in 1747, published a *Plan of the Dictionary*.

1. Johnson expressed the hope that, by registering usage, he could fix the language.

2. The *Plan* uses military imagery, painting the lexicographer as a Caesar who will conquer Britain and regulate its language.

C. The *Dictionary* took longer to produce than the three years Johnson had predicted in the *Plan*. When it was published in 1755, the *Dictionary* included a preface in which Johnson explained that his plan to fix the language was unrealizable.

   1. He had come to recognize that language was mutable, in flux. As we saw in the quotation from Caxton, English lies under the "domyunancioun of the moone." For Johnson, language was "sublunary": mutable and transitory.

   2. Thus, Johnson recognized that his goal was not to fix but "to register" the language.

   3. Johnson also recorded in his preface his recognition of the immensity of his project. The job of the lexicographer is not so much colonial and imperial as it is mythical: "...to persue perfection was, like the first inhabitants of Arcadia, to chace the sun, which, when they had reached the hill where he seemed to rest, was still beheld at the same distance from them."

IV. What were Johnson's innovations in the *Dictionary*? How is the *Dictionary* a testament to this Johnsonian sense of linguistic mutability and flexibility? How is it as much a work of autobiography as it is a work of lexicography?

A. Johnson's syntheses and innovations in lexicography are many.

   1. His was the first dictionary for the general reader rather than the specialist. It was not a list of "hard words" from new sciences; rather, it sought to bring together the best in the study of the history of English to date in a book designed for the literate individual.

   2. In typical 18th-century fashion, Johnson surveyed and synthesized what he considered to be the best and most representative about his subject, limiting his selection to about 40,000 words of general usage. The challenge, of course, was in defining "words of general usage."

B. One of the great achievements of Johnson's *Dictionary* is the use of aphoristic definitions. Examples include the following:

   1. *Network*: "Anything reticulated or decussated, at equal distances, with interstices between the intersections." Is the use of such complex words here a case of Johnsonian humor or irony, or is it meant to give the reader a sense of the infinite regress of language—the idea that word provokes word?

   2. *Cough*: "A convulsion of the lungs, vellicated by some sharp serosity."

   3. *Oats*: "A grain which in England is generally given to horses, but in Scotland appears to support the people."

   4. *Lexicographer*: "A writer of dictionaries; a harmless drudge that busies himself in tracing the original and detailing the signification of words."

C. Johnson, however, was more an aesthetician of the word than a harmless drudge, and his *Dictionary* was written for the reader who would aspire to "exactness of criticism or elegance of style."

   1. Unlike his predecessors, Johnson did not argue for a class-oriented diction or, necessarily, for education as the primary criterion for language use. Rather, he argued for aesthetics—for judgment of the beauty, exactness, and elegance of language.

   2. Not just a synthesis, the *Dictionary* is a work that articulates the distinctive 18th-century idea of synthesis itself: an ideal of discovering what had proved to be the most generally durable or characteristic quality in things, and then to profit by using that quality as a standard working basis. Johnson thus attempted to find the best in English usage in his day and to sanction or stabilize it.

   3. But Johnson rejected the idea of a national institution that would legislate language usage on the model of the French Académie Française or the Italian Accademia della Crusca. He repeatedly said that language is mutable.

D. In the *Dictionary*, we can see Johnson's interest in the debate concerning the use of figurative versus literal definitions.

Should such words as *flagrant* or *ardent* be defined literally as "on fire" or "burning," or should their definitions encompass their figurative meanings of "emotionally charged" or "excited"?

E. Even though he does not highlight class explicitly as a marker of linguistic usage, Johnson was conscious of class and register in language. His definitions often signal whether a word is "low" or affected.

    1. For example, his definition of *chaperone* reads: "An affected word of very recent introduction." Johnson didn't like the word because it is French.

    2. The words Johnson considers "low" include those that sound bad to his ear, are repetitive, or are evocative of the social class from which they emerge: *swap, wobble, budge, coax, twittle-twattle.*

    3. In this way, Johnson provides his readers with a guide to usage in addition to his definitions.

V. Let's turn to some of Johnson's attitudes toward language and the way in which these attitudes inform some of the technical accomplishments of the dictionary.

A. As we've said, Johnson learned in the course of his project that it would be impossible to fix the language. He derides those lexicographers who would "embalm [the language] and secure [it] from corruption and decay."

B. For Johnson, the arbiters of language were literary and aesthetic writers rather than scientific writers. When he quotes from scientific or nonfiction writers, such as Locke, Newton, or Hume, he selects quotations for their rhetorical or aesthetic value.

C. Everywhere in the *Dictionary*, we find Shakespeare and Milton; Johnson applies the standards of quality and judgment drawn from literary criticism and English literature to standards of language performance in everyday, nonliterary circumstances.

VI. Johnson's *Dictionary* ran through four editions in his own lifetime and many afterward. At the end of the 19th century, when scholars in England set out to create a new dictionary (which would eventually become the *Oxford English*

Dictionary), they originally called it *The New English Dictionary* in deference to Johnson's, which was the Old.

A. Johnson's *Dictionary* regularized the spellings of words, ordered words alphabetically, codified the spelling reforms of the 17th and 18th centuries, and broadened the vocabulary of everyday speech.

B. Johnson also established the reliance on literature as a basis for linguistic usage. For Johnson, great authors are linguistic innovators, and the history of literature is, therefore, the history of the language.

C. Johnson sought to excise slang and colloquialism from polite speech by distinguishing classes of words that he called "low." This, in turn, made it possible for individuals to educate themselves using the *Dictionary*.

D. Johnson's was the first dictionary used in the home and the first to be reprinted in smaller versions to make it affordable for personal use. The idea of the dictionary as a social necessity, as well as a linguistic one, originated with Johnson. As we will see in future lectures, the dictionary will, in fact, become both an arbiter of language and a guide to life.

Reading:

Robert DeMaria, *Johnson's Dictionary and the Language of Learning*.

Alan Reddick, *The Making of Johnson's Dictionary*.

W. K. Wimsatt, *Philosophic Words: A Study of Style and Meaning in the Rambler and Dictionary of Samuel Johnson*.

Questions to Consider:

1. In what ways does Samuel Johnson's *Dictionary* differ from previous lexicographies in English?

2. How does Johnson's *Dictionary* differ from most standard dictionaries today?

Lecture Twenty-One—Transcript
Samuel Johnson and His *Dictionary*

The remarkable rise in the vocabulary of English provoked many changes to the language. In my previous lectures, I tried to call attention to the way in which such phenomena as inkhorn terms, aureate diction, Renaissance rhetoric, and the influx of words from technology, colonialization, travel, and science had all radically increased the word stock of the English language.

But I also tried to suggest that a larger attitude change was at work in English. In other words, that what we see in the period from 1500 to 1700 is not simply a raw increase in the number of words, but a change in social attitude—that is, the English language and its speakers become omnivorous, or voracious, in their appetite for new words, and the number of words increases rapidly—new coinages and new phrases.

What I'm going to look at in this and in the following lecture are some of the ways in which scholars and critics, readers and writers, responded to this remarkable rise in vocabulary by developing several tools, guides, or interpretive matrices for that vocabulary. And, of course, the most obvious one is the dictionary.

I want to begin this lecture by looking at some issues in dictionary-making—looking at the origins of lexicography and the ways in which the dictionaries of so-called "hard words," at the beginning of the 16th and 17th centuries, give rise to larger problems of lexicography and larger projects such as Samuel Johnson's great dictionary of 1755.

Let's begin with the origins of the dictionary. The earliest dictionaries in English—and by this I mean not dictionaries from one language to another, because certainly there were dictionaries of Latin and there were dictionaries of modern languages long before there were dictionaries just of English—the earliest English dictionaries are, as far as we can tell, lists of what were called "hard word." In other words, they were guides to the new coinages or to the language that was coming in from science, trade, and exploration.

John Bullokar published his *Expositor* in 1616. Among the many disciplines that he lists on his title page, are what he calls words from "logic, law, physics and astronomy." So a book like the *Expositor* is a guidebook to technology—a list of polysyllabic words.

In 1623, the *Dictionarie of Cockeram* had words for—and here I also quote, from his title page: "Birds, beasts, boyes, critics, cities, destinies," and so on.

By 1658 the *New World of Words* of Phillips—I want to stress this title here—lists on its title page 41 arts and sciences from which its words are taken. I want to stress that in a phrase like "the new world of words," and in the title pages of these dictionaries, what we see are, if you like, the lexicographical equivalents of the great journeys of exploration and colonization. The language of colonial enterprise is going to inform the language of lexicography.

Later in this lecture, when we look at Samuel Johnson's own work in the middle of the 18th century, we're going to see how this notion of colonialization—this notion of, if you like, military and scientific conquest—corresponds to a notion of lexicographical and verbal conquest.

What are these old books like? A characteristic of these early dictionaries was an attention to the details of technology. In 1736, Nathaniel Bailey published his *Dictionary* of what he called "hard and technical words, or terms of art." On his title page, he lists 62 separate arts, sciences, and—I find this fascinating—what he calls "mysteries."

What Bailey did was he did not simply list these strange new or developing words, what he also included were familiar words. He set out to organize his definitions in particular, if you like, hierarchical form. He was interested in word histories, he was interested in etymology, and he was also interested in the relationship between figurative expression and literal expression. One of the things that emerges from Bailey's *Dictionary*, and one of the things that emerges for lexicographers in the 18th century across the board, is whether one should privilege the figurative meaning over the literal meaning, even if that old literal meaning has passed out of use.

This is going to be one of the central questions for Samuel Johnson. Samuel Johnson, 1709–1784, was a lexicographer, a literary critic, a poet, and an essayist. He was the tastemaker to his generation. In addition to his famous work on the *Dictionary*, he wrote a variety of critical, interpretive, and poetic works that give voice to a vision of the world. That vision of the world is psychological and it is aesthetic.

Johnson is preoccupied with notions of transitoriness and mutability. One of his poems is called "The Vanity of Human Wishes," and one of his major works, *Rasselas*, a bit of prose fiction, is very much keyed to this idea of the mutable and the vain. But what Johnson was *also* concerned about was the question of whether or not particular works of literature and particular texts in the English language would have an afterlife. In other words, were these works things that were going to survive, and how could he, as a critic, create not just a canon of authorship but a canon of language?

What's going on in Johnson's *Dictionary* and how does it begin? The idea of the *Dictionary* really begins in the 1740s, and Johnson is concerned with finding a patron. He finds a patron in the great Lord Chesterfield. And in 1747, he publishes what he calls a *Plan of the Dictionary*. He dedicates it to his patron, Lord Chesterfield, and he believes that in about three years he could produce a dictionary of the English language.

His goal in the plan is to express the belief that by registering usage, he will fix the language. The idea here—to go back to our earlier discussion of prescriptivism versus descriptivism—was that Johnson believed that by describing the language in a particular way and by passing judgment on its forms and idioms, he could fix it. In the *Plan of the Dictionary*, he writes to Lord Chesterfield—and I want to read you some selections from the *Plan*, because they're fascinating for the rhetoric of lexicography. "When I survey the Plan," Johnson wrote, "which I have laid before you," and here he is addressing Chesterfield,

> I cannot, my Lord, but confess, that I am frighted at its extent, and, like the soldiers of Caesar, look on Britain as a new world, which it is almost madness to invade. But I hope, that though I should not complete the conquest, I shall at least discover the coast, civilize part of the inhabitants, and make it easy for some other adventurer to proceed farther, to reduce them wholly to subjection, and settle them under laws.

Look at the imagery here, the idea of the lexicographer like Caesar conquering Britain, and that the English language is like some intractable group of people who must be settled, subjected and regulated under law.

He goes on:

> This, my Lord, is my idea of an English dictionary, a dictionary by which the pronunciation of our language may be fixed, and its attainment facilitated; by which its purity may be preserved, its use ascertained, and its duration lengthened.

The goal of the *Plan* is to create a dictionary that will fix and regulate the English language, and that it will do so not just through techniques of recording usage, pronunciation, and grammar, but that it will do so as part and parcel of a larger imperial enterprise—an image in which Johnson sees himself as something of a Caesar of the word.

The *Dictionary* took longer than the three years Johnson projected; it was not until 1755 that the *Dictionary* was finally published. Here, in the Preface to his great *Dictionary*, Johnson realizes that his plan to fix the language was unrealizable. What he recognizes is that language is mutable and in flux. Like Caxton, who saw English lying under the "domyunancioun of the moone," Johnson saw the English language as, what he called, sublunary—mutable and transitory.

In the Preface of 1755, Johnson recognized that his goal could not be to form, but as he says, "to register" the language. So what I would like to do is share with you a couple of Johnsonian moments from the Preface—moments when he sees language as living; moments when he sees the language as a landscape, for example. When he says that the language is akin to trees in a storm, and trying to fix the language would be like trying to control them. It would be like trying to rope in a river.

One magnificent quotation from the Preface that I'd like to read to you is a moment when Johnson realizes not so much the futility, but the immensity of his project. He says:

> I saw that one enquiry only gave occasion to another, that book referred to book, that to search was not always to find, and to find was not always to be informed; and that thus to

pursue perfection, was, like the first inhabitants of Arcadia, to chase the sun, which, when they had reached the hill where he seemed to rest, was still beheld at the same distance from them.

There is a sense here for the *Dictionary* that Johnson recognizes the mutability of the English language. He recognizes the futility of trying to fix it and he also recognizes—using a different set of metaphors—that the job of the lexicographer is really not so much colonial and imperial, as it is almost mythical.

What's going on in the *Dictionary* itself? What does he innovate? What does he borrow, and how is the *Dictionary* a testament to this Johnsonian sense of linguistic mutability and flexibility? How is it as much a work of autobiography as it is a work of lexicography? Let me begin by saying that Johnson's syntheses and innovations are really many. His is the first dictionary for the general reader, rather than for the specialist—that is, it is not a list of "hard words" from new sciences, rather it is designed as a book for the individual, for the literate, for purchase. It sought to bring together what Johnson thought of as the best in the study of the history of the language to that date.

A characteristic 18th-century critical attitude was to survey and synthesize and then draw from that synthesis the best and most representative, whether it be in criticism, or science, or in this case, lexicography. Johnson limited his selection to about 40,000 words of general usage. The challenge of a dictionary like this is defining words of general usage. It's actually easier to define "hard words" than it is to define everyday words.

One of the great achievements of Johnson's *Dictionary* is the creation of aphoristic definitions. Let me give you some examples of these aphoristic definitions. If I were to say to you, "How do you define common words like *net* or *network*? How do you define a word like *cough* or *oats*; or how do you define a word like *lexicographer*?" you might be hard-pressed, because so many of these words seem so straightforward.

If you look up *network* in Johnson's *Dictionary*, you get this magnificent definition, and I quote, "Anything reticulated or decussated, at equal distances, with interstices between the intersections." This is probably as good a definition of *network* as you're going to get, but the definition uses words far harder and far more complex than the word being defined. Is this a case of Johnsonian humor or irony—and it may well be—or is it also a recognition that part of the challenge of the *Dictionary* lies in the way in which every definition generates a multiplicity of words.

To go back to the lines of the Preface, as he says, "I saw that one enquiry only gave occasion to another, that book referred to book, that to search was not always to find." So what Johnson is doing in these definitions is he's giving, I think, the reader the sense of, if you like, the infinite regress of language—that word provokes word.

Take a word like *cough*: "A convulsion of the lungs, vellicated by some sharp serosity." That's one of my favorites. *Oats* he defines as, "A grain which in England is generally given to horses, but in Scotland appears to support the people." So here is, of course, a little bit of political jabbing and a little bit of Johnsonian wit. Of course when you look up *lexicographer*, you get, "A writer of dictionaries; a harmless drudge that busies himself in tracing the original and detailing the signification of words."

Was Johnson simply a harmless drudge? The drudgery of the *Dictionary* lies not simply in collecting words and illustrative definitions, it also leads to more ambitious goals. Johnson is really an aesthetician of the word. It seems to me that the precise goal of the *Dictionary* is an education in aesthetics. This *Dictionary*, he says, is written for that reader who would aspire to, "exactness of criticism or elegance of style."

Unlike his predecessors, Johnson did not argue for a class-oriented diction; he did not argue for a dialect based on region; he did not even argue, necessarily, for education as the primary criterion for language use. Rather, Johnson really argued for aesthetics—for judgment of the beauty, as he says, exactness and elegance. So his illustrative examples and his definitions are really keyed in the end to questions of aesthetic.

As I mentioned earlier, the *Dictionary* is a work that articulates this distinctive 18th-century idea of synthesis itself—that is, an ideal of discovery; what had proved to be the most generally durable or characteristic quality in things—and then to profit by using that quality as a standard working basis. So Johnson attempted to find the best in English usage of his day and to sanction and to stabilize it. But Johnson does not want to legislate language.

One of the discussions and debates that was going on in the 17th and 18th centuries was whether there should be a national academy of language. The French have the Académie Française, the Italian have the Accademia della Crusca. Many writers of the 17th and 18th centuries weighed in on whether there should be a national or royal academy of language. Johnson rejected that idea because, as he said, we cannot legislate language, as he put it, when we see men grow old and die. We recognize, as he said again and again, that language itself is mutable, that new words are coming in from science and art, that polysemy is constantly at work, and that certain words are changing meaning.

I mentioned earlier in this lecture and in my previous lectures how one of the central debates was the relationship between the figurative and the literal. One of the central questions of that debate was precisely whether one should define words, as he says, like *flagrant* and *ardent* as meaning literally "on fire" or "burning," or more figuratively, "emotionally charged," or "excited," which were the common definitions of the time. We can see that Johnson is interested in the way in which these particular ranges of words are going on.

Johnson, even though he is not using class explicitly as a marker of linguistic usage, is very conscious of class and register in language. One of the things that Johnson does in his definitions is he will very often signal whether a word is "low," or colloquial, or slang. "Low" is one of his judgment words, if you like. Another is "affectation." He says, for example, for the word *chaperone*, he says "An affected word of very recent introduction." He doesn't like it because it's French.

By contrast, Johnson identifies a set of words that he considers "low," and these words are really, again, not grounded so much in vulgarity or content as they are in aesthetics. Johnson doesn't like words that sound bad. He doesn't like words that are repetitive, that are onomatopoetic, or that are evocative of the social class from which they come. Here are some Johnsonian "low" words: *swap, wobble, budge, coax, twittle-twattle.*

What Johnson is doing is he's providing his reader not only with definitions, but he's providing his reader with a guide to usage. As a dictionary today enables readers to figure out the appropriate word for a given moment, so Johnson's *Dictionary*, in its own time, was designed to do that. In this he reminds us of so many of the 17th- and 18th-century scholars that we've seen before.

What I'd like to turn to now is a set of, if you like, Johnsonian attitudes towards language and the way in which Johnson's attitudes towards language inform some of the technical accomplishments of the dictionary.

I had mentioned the issue of mutability, and I repeatedly talked about Johnson's sense of transitoriness and vanity. In the Preface to the *Dictionary*, he talks about how we must laugh at the elixir that promises to prolong life a thousand years. Therefore, he derides those lexicographers who would embalm their language and secure them from corruption and decay. This reminds us, of course, of the imagery of the *Plan*, where he wanted, "to preserve the purity," as he said, of English. Now he recognizes that this is impossible.

Johnson recognizes that technical meanings become figurative; he recognizes that words are classed by register. And so the arbiters of language for Johnson are going to be literary and aesthetic writers rather than, necessarily, scientific writers. Even when Johnson quotes from scientific or nonfiction writers like Locke or like Newton or like Hume, he's selecting quotations for their rhetorical or their aesthetic value.

We can see here in so many ways that Johnson's achievement is to select quotations from—how can I put it?—from the best, from the most exact in literature and in culture. If you look through Johnson's *Dictionary*, certain writers will rise to the surface. Shakespeare is everywhere in Johnson. Milton's *Paradise Lost* is everywhere in the *Dictionary*. John Locke and David Hume are everywhere in the *Dictionary*. You can see here in the kind of uses and the selections that Johnson's doing, you can see how he is creating not just a canon of words, but a canon of texts.

What Johnson is doing is he is applying the standards of quality and judgment drawn from literary criticism and English literature to standards of language performance in everyday nonliterary circumstances. This is, it seems to me, the primary Johnsonian innovation in lexicography. Reading through the *Dictionary*, you can recognize these forms. But reading through the *Dictionary* you can also see Johnson once again.

And I want to turn, before my summary, to one last extended quotation from the Preface—the sense of the Johnsonian life here. "It is the fate of those," he says at the beginning of his Preface to the *Dictionary*:

> … who toil at the lower employments of life, to be rather driven by the fear of evil, than attracted by the prospect of good; to be exposed to censure, without hope of praise; to be disgraced by miscarriage, or punished for neglect, where success would have been without applause, and diligence without reward.

> Among these unhappy mortals is the writer of dictionaries; whom mankind have considered, not as the pupil, but the slave of science, the pionier [*sic*] of literature; doomed only to remove rubbish and clear obstructions from the paths of learning and Genius, who press forward to conquest and glory, without bestowing a smile on the humble drudge that facilitates their progress. Every other author may aspire to praise; the lexicographer can only hope to escape reproach. And even this negative recompense has yet been granted to very few.

Whatever is at stake in Johnson's emotional condition, the fact remains that his *Dictionary* of 1755 did not simply escape reproach, but was something of great praise. It ran through four editions in his own lifetime, and it ran through many editions afterward. Indeed, the impact of Johnson's *Dictionary* was so great that the scholars around the philological society of England at the end of the 19th century, when they set out to create a new dictionary—what would eventually become the *Oxford English Dictionary*—they originally called it *The New English Dictionary*, because Johnson's was the Old.

Let me summarize some of Johnson's achievements and look forward to some of the issues in my next lecture when I'll talk about the location of Johnson's work in the larger context of 18th- and 19th-century theories of language and language teaching. Johnson's *Dictionary* regularized the spellings of words. He ordered them alphabetically, he preferred certain spellings over others, and he codified the spelling reforms of the 17th- and 18th-century grammarians that I had talked about in my previous lectures.

He brought in the vocabulary of everyday speech—that is, even though Johnson limited his *Dictionary* to 40,000 words, what he did do was that by including those words, by giving them aphoristic definitions and by using quotations from the great writers of English literature and English intellectual life to illustrate them, he made the words part of everyday speech.

He also established the reliance on literature. So the quotations from great writers and from relatively unfamiliar writers, too, enter the canon in ways that Johnson's *Dictionary* becomes a testimony to his own reading, but it also becomes an anthology for later readers as well. Literary history becomes linguistic history, and—and this will, I think, become a central theme for not just this course, but for all of our reading of literature—what Johnson's *Dictionary* does is it has as its implicit argument the notion that great authors are linguistic innovators, and that the history of literature is therefore the history of the English language.

Johnson also sought to excise slang and colloquialism from polite speech by distinguishing classes of words that he called "low." And he also, therefore, made it possible for individuals, in effect, to educate themselves by using the *Dictionary*. The dictionary becomes now, for the first time, an arbiter of linguistic social life.

As I mentioned, Johnson's influence on the OED was profound, and his influence on later lexicography was remarkable. Certainly the influence, it seems to me, is not simply in his words, but in the status of the dictionary as a book. Johnson's *Dictionary* is really the first dictionary that's in the home. It's the first dictionary to be reprinted and published in ways after Johnson's lifetime that make it affordable. There are many, many copies of early editions of the *Dictionary* which are abbreviated or abridged—many copies not in the great large folio books of the original publication, but in much smaller home-bookshelf sizes—so that the idea of "look it up in the dictionary," the very notion of the dictionary as a social, as well as a linguistics, necessity, originates with Johnson.

With Johnson, we can see, then, that synthesis that I have been building towards—that is, the way in which an increasing vocabulary in English, changes in pronunciation and spelling, and debates on pedagogy and the politics of language come to be codified into a handbook for social experience and language.

As we will see in my next lecture, the larger issues of propriety itself, as a grammatical as well as a social category, inform the cultural perspectives of the late 18th and early 19th century, and lead us to an understanding of how the dictionary becomes both an arbiter of language and a guide to life.

Lecture Twenty-Two
New Standards in English

Scope:

The rise of lexicography and the success of *Johnson's Dictionary* fed into the larger debate about prescriptivism and descriptivism in language study and teaching. In this lecture, we examine several influential writers from the later 18th century who crystallize the debate. In addition, we will look at several words that are changing meaning during this period and that reflect the larger cultural problem of linguistic usage and social behavior. Who we are and how we speak and write are questions asked at the close of the 18th century in ways that remarkably anticipate our own debates.

Outline

I. As we saw in the last lecture, Samuel Johnson's *Dictionary* had an immense impact on the scholarship of the English language. It also participated in a larger set of debates about the nature of language study and teaching.

    A. We've touched on the issue of prescriptivism and descriptivism at several points in this course. The central question here is: Should we study language in order to provide instruction in what we should say and write, or should the goal be simply to describe existing forms of language behavior?

    B. The paradox, of course, is that in describing language, almost any authority invariably prescribes language behavior, as well.

II. Two figures of the 18th century who exemplify the debate on prescriptivism versus descriptivism are Robert Lowth and Joseph Priestley.

    A. Lowth was bishop of London. Educated at Oxford, he was a key figure in the religious and educational establishment in England in the second half of the 18th century.

        1. He was the author of many works on language, including *Principles of English Grammar* (1762, revised 1787).

2. Lowth was clearly a prescriptivist. In *Principles*, he remarked that his goal was "To teach what is right by teaching what is right and wrong."

3. In another work, *A Short Introduction to English Grammar*, he defined grammar itself as "The art of rightly expressing our thoughts in words."

4. Lowth held that whatever difficulties may exist in communication are the fault of "practice," not of the language itself.

5. What makes Lowth a prescriptivist is his strict notion of right and wrong. Grammar, for Lowth, is not a universal category of making or marking relationships among syntax and meaning, but it is the art of right expression.

6. Lowth was also interested in using Latin as a template for English grammar.

B. Joseph Priestley was a Scot, an empiricist and scientist, one of the discoverers of oxygen, and a founder of Unitarianism. As an experimental scientist, he was a follower of David Hume and was interested in deducing general principles from observation.

1. Priestley was the author of *Rudiments of English Grammar* (1761, revised in 1772, and reprinted frequently thereafter). He considered grammar not an essential quality of language but "a collection of observations on the structure of it, and a system of rules for the proper use of it."

2. One of the key features of British empiricism in the 18th century was a belief in simplicity; that is, that nature at its most natural was simple. Thus, Priestley favored eliminating those aspects of the English language that were not simple, including "Gallicisms" (French words).

3. Priestley wrote of the "true idiom of the English language" and the "genius of our language." Although these terms might seem loaded, what Priestley is really looking for is the heart of the language, the features that make English most characteristically English.

4. He considered the study of language as a system of empirical observation, but given his involvement with the religious and political controversies of his day, he also offered a political edge to language study: "I think it

not only unsuitable to the genius of a free nation but in itself ill-calculated to reform and fix a language."

III. The idea of propriety in linguistic and social behavior came to the fore at around the same time as this debate.

   A. The word *propriety* comes from the same Latin root as the word *proper*. Both of them are related to the idea of "belonging to." The term developed from a word of physical or commercial use, to one of linguistic use, to one of social action. In this, it serves as an example of *extension in lexis*, the movement of a word from a highly technical and specific definition to a set of larger, more figurative, and social definitions.

   B. Johnson's *Dictionary* offers the following definitions of *propriety*:
      1. "Peculiarity of possession, exclusive right."
      2. "Accuracy, justness, especially in a linguistic sense." Here, Johnson also offers a quotation from the philosopher John Locke: "Common sense, that is the rule of propriety, affords some aid to settle the signification of language."

   C. Thus, in mid-18th-century usage, propriety was a grammatical rather than a social issue. The term could mean accuracy of expression, but it also referred to the use of proper grammatical forms or endings.
      1. Only by extension does the word take on a stylistic and social connotation, but this was an important cultural shift: What is grammatically proper becomes socially acceptable.
      2. In Lowth's *Principles*, the word is used in the phrase "the rule of propriety" to mean grammatical concord in making "the signification of language" meaningful. Lowth uses the term only in its relation to grammar in his highly technical discussions of the subjunctive mood.
      3. In the preface to his *Dictionary* of 1755, Johnson wrote that the illiterate "forget propriety" in their speech or writing, meaning that they write awkwardly or ungrammatically.
      4. Over time, however, these grammatical issues became social issues. By 1784, Fanny Burney, one of the great

arbiters of late-18th-century taste, could write: "Such propriety of mind as can only result from the union of good sense and virtue." Good sense and virtue are now matters of propriety, and in turn, grammatical performance is associated with social accomplishment.

D. In late-18th-century literature, propriety became the marker of exactly this nexus of linguistic, social, and moral behavior.

    1. Thomas Sterne's *Sentimental Journey* of 1762 uses the term precisely in its modern social sense.

    2. In the novels of Jane Austen, we see how verbal performance becomes the marker of social accomplishment and, in turn, generates "the union of good sense and virtue."

IV. Along with this debate on proprietary, a larger debate took place on slang and colloquialism.

  A. As mentioned in the last lecture, Johnson identified some words as "low" or improper in his *Dictionary*, largely because they had a certain aesthetic cacophony. *Swap*, *twittle-twattle*, *wobble*, *budge*, *coax*, and *touchy* are examples. Johnson also objected to *chaperone*, which he described as "affected."

  B. The legacy of such examples can be found in our own dictionaries today, where we see the arbitration of linguistic use in the details of definitions.

    1. Examples include obvious words, such as *ain't*, which most of us have been taught is inappropriate.

    2. We find a less obvious example in the emphasis placed on the French origin of the word *protocol* by the *Oxford English Dictionary*. Even in this modern dictionary, we see the 18th-century tendency to mark certain words as alien or un-English.

    3. The definition of *quiz* in the Oxford English Dictionary is even more emphatic in highlighting that word's dubious linguistic propriety: "Of obscure origin, possibly a fanciful coinage, but it is doubtful whether any reliance can be placed on the anecdote of its invention by Daly, a Dublin theatre-manager."

C. *Quiz* and *protocol* represent words that have entered everyday speech in almost transparent ways, but their history and lexicography show the legacies of prescriptivism and descriptivism.

Reading:

Albert C. Baugh and Thomas Cable, *A History of the English Language*.

Robert DeMaria, *Johnson's Dictionary and the Language of Learning*.

Ruth Mack, "The Historicity of Johnson's Lexicographer." *Representations* 76.

J. A. H. Murray, et al., *The Oxford English Dictionary*.

Questions to Consider:

1. How did Robert Lowth and Joseph Priestley fundamentally differ in their beliefs about language?

2. What is the role of propriety in the debate over English usage today?

Lecture Twenty-Two—Transcript
New Standards in English

Samuel Johnson's *Dictionary* had an immense impact on the teaching, study, and scholarship of the English language in the decades after its publication. In 1755, the original publication of the *Dictionary* and in its many subsequent editions throughout the 18th and the 19th century, Samuel Johnson's *Dictionary* quite simply became *the* dictionary of the English language.

But as I suggested in my previous lecture, *Johnson's Dictionary* participates in a larger set of debates about the nature of language study and teaching. What I'd like to do in this lecture is focus on a couple of contemporaries of Samuel Johnson to illustrate one of the central tensions of the time, and to link that tension to a larger arc in the theme of this course as a whole.

That theme is the relationship between prescriptivism and descriptivism. Should the study of language prescribe behavior? Should we study language in order to instruct us in what we should say, or should the study of language be largely descriptive? Should our goal be simply to describe forms of behavior that are out there? The paradox of description, however, is the paradox of recognizing that whenever you describe something—depending on your authority or your position, or your rhetorical control—you will almost invariably prescribe something. If you are of enough power or authority, or if you put it in a memorable way, you're description becomes a prescription.

Even though Johnson recognized in the Preface to his *Dictionary* that it was impossible to form or fix or register a language, nonetheless, the immense authority and brilliance of the dictionary itself made it an arbiter of linguistic usage for over a century after its publication.

Two figures of the 18th century who exemplify the debate on prescriptivism versus descriptivism, are Robert Lowth and Joseph Priestley. Lowth and Priestley were both engaged not only in the linguistic discussions of their time, but on the social and religious debates of the last half of the 18th century. So they may exemplify some aspects of English intellectual culture as well as English linguistic and literary study.

Robert Lowth was Bishop of London. He was educated at Oxford, and he was a key figure in the religious and the educational establishment in England in the second half of the 18th century. He was the author of many works on language, including his *Principles of English Grammar*, which first appeared in 1762, and which was revised in 1787. Lowth was clearly a prescriptivist.

In his *Principles*, he remarked that his goal was, "To teach what is right by teaching what is right and wrong." And so grammar, he believed, was a system of rules. In his work called, *A Short Introduction to English Grammar*, Lowth defined grammar itself as, "… the art of rightly expressing our thoughts in words." He believed, in fact, that English grammar was the best of all. Of all the European languages, he said, "English is much the most simple in its form and construction." Lowth held that whatever difficulties may exist in communication, were the fault of what he called practice, and not of the language itself. He blamed people's lack of what he called propriety and accuracy to teach what is right by showing what is both right and wrong.

What makes Lowth a prescriptivist is this notion of the axes of right and wrong. Grammar, for Lowth, is not a universal category of making or marking relationships among syntax and meaning, nor is it a habit of mind. It is an art of right expression. And common principles are applied to a particular language according to accepted forms of usage and custom.

One cannot but look back on Lowth from our perspective and see in his establishment qualities—in his place in the English establishment—a sense of the desire to establish grammatical categories and rules. Even though Lowth holds that English grammar was as he says, much the most simple, nonetheless, as a figure of the ecclesiastical and political establishment, he wants to use Latin as a template for that grammar.

One of the things he does in great detail in many of his grammatical and pedagogical works is he tries to make the paradigms of English nouns and verbs correspond to the paradigms of Latin nouns and verbs. So you have cases or you have declensions or you have conjugations that are organized on Latin models.

I want to contrast Lowth with Joseph Priestley. Joseph Priestley was not an Englishman, but he was a Scot. He was an empiricist, he was a scientist, he was, in fact, one of the discoverers of the element oxygen. He was the founder of Unitarianism. As an experimental scientist and as an empiricist, he was a follower of his fellow Scotsman, David Hume, and he was very interested in deducing general principles from observation.

He said things like, "Language, like water, will seek its own natural level." Among the things he wrote on language were what he called the *Rudiments of English Grammar*, which was first published in 1761, revised in 1772, and published frequently thereafter. Priestley considered grammar not as an essential quality of language, but as what he called, "a collection of observations on the structure of it, and a system of rules for the proper use of it."

This is a very important distinction from Lowth's—that the idea here is that grammar is "a collection of observations on the structure of [language]" rather than an art of rightly expressing thoughts and words. Priestley's concern is looking at the world out there and deducing general principals from it. So he applies his empiricist scientific methodology to the study of language itself.

Part of this, of course, is not without its value judgments. One of the key features of British empiricism of the 18th century, and a good deal of the experimental science that emerged from it, was a belief in simplicity—that is, that nature at its most natural was simple, and that the laws of nature or that the equations that governed those laws were to be reduced to their most simple form. This is, just as an aside it seems to me, one of the still-controlling aesthetic principles of science—the idea that there is something aesthetically beautiful in the simple equation, and that nature's laws, if we could only understand them, would be revealed as truly simple.

What Priestley favored was the elimination of those aspects of the English language that he thought made it not simple. He favored the elimination of what he called "gallicisms" from language—that is, forms of French—big words. He was interested in finding what he called the "true idiom of the English language," and what he called the "genius of the language."

I think it's important to recognize that even though these are loaded terms—and even though these would make us believe that what Priestley is talking about is something like the English language is somehow better than all others, or the sense that there is a purer

©2008 The Teaching Company.

English than any other—what we need to understand is that he's really talking about the English language in the way he's talking about nature. That is, he wants to get to the heart of it. He wants to find the true genius by which he means not genius in the modern sense of brilliant people—he wants to find the origin. He wants to find what makes English most characteristically English in the way that one looks for what is most characteristic in, let's say, a species or in a chemical reaction.

He considered the study of language as a system of empirical observation, but as someone who was intimately involved in the religious and political controversies of his day, he offers a political edge to language study. Here is a quotation that I have gotten from the 1772 edition of the *Rudiments of English Grammar*. I want to read it to you because I think it is a profoundly resonant statement for the history of language. He writes, "I think it not only unsuitable to the genius of a free nation but in itself ill-calculated to reform and fix a language."

Look at this language: "the genius of a free nation." Priestley, who would eventually travel to America and bring Unitarianism to America, is working in a word in which discussions of language are always political, and where the notion of "nation" is central to the understanding of language itself. In 1772, a phrase like, "the genius of a free nation," must resonate with the incipient debates on the status of the American colonies, with the relationship between kingship and common profit, and with notions of ill-calculation to reform and fix a language. Reform now, as a matter of social and political reform; calculation now, not simply as a matter of toting of the numbers on the board of life, but of reckoning-up the taxation and representation that would be so much a key feature of the American rebellion of the 1770s.

I want to stress here, the end of the 18th century, the profound political resonances of debates on prescriptivism and descriptivism at the very moment of American rebellion.

One of the key issues, also, that emerges from this debate is not simply the matter of grammatical correctness—what is right and what is wrong—and also not only the issue of political control, but matters of social behavior. In other words, what is proper and what is improper. The word *propriety* comes to develop at the end of the 18th century as one of the touchstone words for linguistic and social behavior, and I would like to spend some time looking now at propriety.

Propriety is a remarkable word and we can use the resources of 18th-century lexicography and linguistic criticism to understand its remarkable qualities. The word *propriety* comes, of course, from the same Latin root as the word *proper*. Both of them go back to an idea of belonging to—something that is one's own; something that is, in fact, a matter of propriety.

The term developed from words for physical or commercial use, and then it became one of linguistic use, and then it became one of social action. I've talked about this process in earlier lectures as extension in lexis—that is, the way in which a word moves from a highly-technical and specific definition to a set of larger, more figurative and social definitions.

When you look up the word *propriety* in Johnson's *Dictionary*, in the first edition of 1755, what you get is the following definition: first, "Peculiarity of possession, exclusive right." You're not getting a social definition here. Propriety is not how you behave well in a particular situation. Propriety is about owning something—exclusive right. Definition two is, "Accuracy, justness, especially in a linguistic sense." Here, Johnson offers a quotation from one of his most favorite arbiters of language and philosophy, the late-17th-and early-18th-century philosopher, John Locke. Here is the quotation from Locke that Johnson uses to illustrate his definition two of *propriety*. "Common sense, that is the rule of propriety, affords some aid to settle the signification of language."

What *propriety* means here is a grammatical, rather than a social issue. It can mean accuracy of expression, but what it also means is the use of proper grammatical forms or endings. In other words, that when 18th-century writers write about propriety in language, what they're talking about, for example, is concord between a noun and a verb—that is, making sure that if you have a plural noun, you use a plural verb; or making sure that there are certain case relationships; or making sure that you use the right preposition in a particular phrase. Only by extension does the word *propriety* take on stylistic and social connotation.

What we're looking at the close of the 18th century, is a very important cultural shift. What is grammatically proper becomes socially acceptable. In Lowth's book the *Principles of English Grammar*, he uses the term *propriety* in the following way, "the rule of propriety," as he says means grammatical concord in "making the signification of language meaningful." He's using this in a very special sense.

Lowth was very interested, as I mentioned earlier, in finding ways of describing English grammar in terms of Latin grammar. And Lowth was very concerned, in a very technical discussion with making sure that English could have a subjunctive mood. I've talked about the subjunctive—that is, the counterfactual, or the conditional, or the optative. That is, a way of expressing something that isn't there but you'd like to be there, that might be there. Were I doing something— that's the subjunctive.

Lowth's discussion is highly technical. The point I want to draw from that technical discussion without going into all of the details of his 18th-century pedantry, is the simple fact that the issue of propriety for Lowth is an issue of grammar. It is not an issue of social décor. Gradually, over time, these grammatical issues become social issues. When Johnson writes in the Preface to the *Dictionary* in 1755, that the illiterate "forget propriety" in their speech and writing, what he means is that they write awkwardly or ungrammatically. It does not mean that they are speaking badly in terms of subject matter. The issue is not a subject-matter issue; the issue is a grammar issue.

By 1784, Fanny Burney, novelist, social critic, one of the great arbiters of late-18th-century taste could write, "Such propriety of mind as can only result from the union of good sense and virtue." This is very important because now good sense and virtue are matters of propriety. It seems to me that what's at stake here in Fanny Burney, is precisely the idea of grammatical concord; of technical, grammatical performance as the mark of social accomplishment. *Virtue*, that word *virtue* again, is the moral basis of social behavior.

Recall the way in which *virtue* appeared in the *Canterbury Tales*, of which *vertu engendred is the fleur*. In Middle English and in early Modern English, just as in Latin, virtue is a distinctively masculine category. It has to do with power, and it has to do with the power to engender, quite simply. By the 18th century, virtue is not an inner quality of the man, but an outer quality of the social being. Indeed, virtue comes by the middle of the 18th century, to be associated with female forms of performance—indeed, chastity, that Richardson's great novel *Pamela* can be subtitled "Virtue Rewarded."

In late-18th-century literature, propriety became the marker of exactly this nexus of the social and the moral in behavior. Thomas Sterne's great novella *Sentimental Journey* of 1762 uses the term *propriety* precisely in its modern social sense, but he uses it as if it were a loan word from French. He spells it *propriété*; it is italicized; it is something which as a concept word, he wants to signal as not fully part of English.

If you like, one could write a history of the English novel and one could certainly make an argument for someone like Jane Austen as a novelist of propriety, precisely in this late-18th-century sense—that is, the way in which verbal performance becomes the marker of social accomplishment, and that verbal performance and grammatical ability generates what Fanny Burney called "the union of good sense and virtue."

Along with this debate on propriety is a larger debate on slang and colloquialism. I mentioned in my previous lecture the way in which Johnson, in his *Dictionary*, beginning in its first edition of 1755, signals certain words as improper, by which I'm now meaning improper in its modern sense. Johnson arbitrates certain kinds of words, and I mentioned how low words for Johnson are not simply words that come from the vulgar or words of a particular subject matter, they're words that are socially unacceptable because they sound funny, or they have a certain aesthetic cacophony to them. And I mentioned *swap*, *twittle-twattle*, *wobble*, *budge*, and also words like *coax* and *touchy*—monosyllabic, reduplicating, onomatopoetic terms.

I mentioned also *chaperone*, which he describes as an "affected word of very recent introduction." What we see in this definition is really the origin of our modern sense of affectation—that is, the way in which one can affect behavior. That is, the way in which one acts or speaks in a manner that is unnatural, in a manner that is un-English and is a manner that for so much of British and American narrative is quite simply a manner that is French.

The legacy of examples such as these can be found in our own dictionaries, and I would like to conclude this lecture by looking ahead—by bridging to my next two lectures—and by, in effect, saying when we read a dictionary today, what we are very often looking at is the legacy of these 18th-century lexicographers, teachers, pedagogues, and pedants; the way in which the arbitration of linguistic use can be found in the details of a definition.

We can see this in some obvious places. We can see this in a word like *ain't*. I've always been taught, as I'm sure many of you have been taught, that the word *ain't* is inappropriate. Yet *ain't* was a word of affectation in the novels of Dorothy Sayers when she has Lord Peter Wimsey talk in this way and say, *ain't*, Peter Wimsey will also drop his "g's" in the participles: *goin'* instead of *going*. One of the questions that a discussion like this raises is a question of whether or not we're looking at a kind of affectation of the common, what is the relationship between upper and lower—what later came to be called "U" and "non-U" speech.

But there are more complicated ways of looking at this and perhaps the most fascinating lies in the *Oxford English Dictionary*. You will remember Johnson on *chaperone*, "An affected word of very recent introduction." He doesn't like it because it's French. If you go to the *Oxford English Dictionary*, what you're looking at are strata of work—definitions that were originally written in the 1880s and 1890s, collocations of quotations that were drawn at the beginning of the 20th century. The *Oxford English Dictionary* was published from the early 1880s until the late 1920s; it was put together in complete form in 1933, and there have been subsequent supplements—indeed, the third edition is now online. Yet, in definitions and descriptions, you can see the legacy of judgment.

One of my favorite words to look up in the OED is the word *protocol*, because here, again, you have a word that is part of the vocabulary of social performance. One follows protocol. One follows protocol diplomatically, one follows protocol also scientifically. But if you look at the word *protocol* in the *Oxford English Dictionary*, you get this remarkable quotation which I would like to read for you.

> The history of the sense-development of this word belongs to Medieval Latin and the Romance languages, esp. French; in

the latter it has received very considerable extensions of meaning …

Then the OED lists a set of famous lexicographers. Then it says:

> The word does not appear to have at any time formed part of the English legal vocabulary It is in Scottish from the 16th c. probably under French influence; otherwise used only in reference to foreign countries and their institutions, and as a recognized form of international diplomacy until it's comparatively recent entry into the general vocabulary of English.

This is still the language of Johnson. How do you define a word as English? How do you mark it as something not-English? Clearly here, what the OED wants to say is that the word *protocol* is really French: "The word does not appear to have at any time formed part of the English legal vocabulary." It goes on in long definition after definition, and use after use. It talks about—and here is another part of it:

> The formulary of the etiquette to be observed by the head of state in official ceremonies in France, relations with ambassadors and the like.

The quotations that the OED gives are designed to show you something of the alien or un-English quality of *protocol*. And the reason why I am calling this to your attention is to show you that even in a modern dictionary, we are saddled with the legacy of 18th-century linguistic judgments.

Let me conclude with one other word from the OED, that gives us, again, a narrative of social use and grammatical propriety. This is the word *quiz*. There will be no quiz after this lecture. But if you look up *quiz* in the OED, what you get is:

> … of obscure origin, possibly a fanciful coinage, but it doubtful whether any reliance can be placed on the anecdote of its invention by Daly, a Dublin theatre-manager.

Once again, you have this magnificent moment of linguistic exile, if you like, for if *protocol* should not be admitted into English because it is ultimately a word of French, *quiz* hovers on the very margins of the language because it is a word (a) from Ireland, "Daly, a Dublin theater-manager," and (b) a word of the theater.

The original editors of the *Oxford English Dictionary* at the end of the 19th and the beginning of the 20th centuries could in many of their definitions think of nothing so bad to say about a word, as that it was theatrical—that it came from the theater. In future lectures I will show you in some other words the ways in which the OED eliminates, or judges, or hierarchizes words according to their naturalness or their theatricality.

Quiz and *protocol* represent the kinds of words that have entered everyday speech in almost transparent ways, but when we look at their history and lexicography, what we're looking at are the legacies of prescriptivism and descriptivism, and the recognition that even our most modern dictionaries today still bear the imprint of the 18th-century lexicographers who would chart "low" words and seek to use linguistic categories to regulate social propriety.

Lecture Twenty-Three
Dictionaries and Word Histories

Scope:

Following up on the study of 18th-century language use and dictionary making, we can see the ways in which the *Oxford English Dictionary* chronicles the history of semantic change. But we can also see some of the political or ideological presuppositions behind the making of the OED (and all dictionaries generally) that may invite us to question the objectivity of modern lexicography. This lecture looks at some key words to illustrate the ways in which words change meaning. It then turns to another set of words to illustrate the politics of lexicography and the judgmentalism of the modern dictionary.

Outline

I. In the past two lectures, we've explored a number of topics related to dictionaries, including the origins of dictionaries; Samuel Johnson, the great dictionary maker; the emergence of the dictionary as a book for the home and as an arbiter of behavior; and the tensions between prescriptivism and descriptivism.

   A. In this lecture, we'll look at some words and some aspects of change in meaning to show how we can use a historical dictionary, such as the *Oxford English Dictionary* (OED), to give us insight into principles of semantic change.

   B. Linguists tend to shy away from offering explanations for why particular changes, such as the GVS, took place. Although we can document such changes in great detail, the causes—social pressure, the anatomy of the mouth, contact among languages, and so on—are invariably debatable.

   C. We can, however, provide some contexts for explaining how certain words change their meaning and, perhaps, look forward to how words might change meaning in the future.

II. Let's begin with a set of principles related to semantic change drawn from recent works of linguistic theory and the history of language.

©2008 The Teaching Company.

A. The first of these principles involves the relationship of ambiguity and limitation: If a word or form has two meanings so incompatible that they cause ambiguity, one of the meanings dies out, or more rarely, the form itself becomes obsolete. Homonymy and polysemy are subheadings in this category.

    1. *Homonymy* relates to the idea that speakers will try to avoid confusion and ambiguity in spoken language by limiting the number of possible homonyms. An extreme example is found in the following Old English words: *a* ("ever"), *ae* ("law"), *aeg* ("egg"), *ea* ("water"), *eoh* ("horse"), *ieg* ("island"). The similarities in pronunciation of these words may have been so great that new words were borrowed or existing words were adapted to avoid homonymy.

    2. We've talked about *polysemy* several times, the phenomenon of one word having several meanings, some of which eventually come to overlap. An example is the word *uncouth*, the history of which we can chart with information from the OED. The word *couth* comes from a Germanic root meaning "known."

Meaning of *Uncouth*	Dates of Usage
unknown	Old English–1650
unfamiliar or strange	Old English, now obsolete
strange or unpleasant	1380–present
uncomely, awkward, clumsy	1513–present
rugged, rough	1542–present
uncultured	1694–present

    a. Note how the meaning of *uncouth* moves from a particular condition to a description grounded in that condition. Something that is unknown becomes alien, strange, weird, rugged, rough, and finally, uncultured.

    b. *Couth* has since taken on an imagined status, as in the phrase "He's got no couth." The usage here is completely ahistorical. Future lexicographers may record *couth* as a word emerging in the late 20th century to mean "propriety, ability, culture, knowledge, or skill."

B. Another way in which words change their meaning is through *extension in lexis*, in which metaphorical meanings or figurative senses take over from older technical or literal meanings. Some examples include those shown in the following table.

Example	Original Meaning	Current Meaning
clog	fasten wood to (1398)	encumber by adhesion (1528)
clasp	fasten (1386), enfold (1447)	grip by hand (1583)
brazen	of brass (Old English)	impudent (1573)
bristle	stand up stiff (1480)	become indignant (1549)
broil	burn (1375)	get angry (1561)

1. These new figurative meanings constitute an important problem in semantic change. Johnson recognized it in making his dictionary, and he organized definitions so that the older, primary, or nonmetaphorical meaning came first—even if that meaning was no longer current.

2. The OED follows Johnson's example, recording word definitions historically.

3. Thus, lexicography creates the impression of hierarchies of meaning, even when those hierarchies do not reflect the actual uses of the time. The dictionary gives us, then, a history of words told through the history of semantic change.

C. As we saw with *ain't*, words can also experience *shifts in class*; in other words, meanings and usages might not change, but class affiliations or registers of meaning might.

1. In the 18th century, *ain't* was used by polite society, frequently in the form of *ant*; the OED considers *ain't* a "later and more illiterate form of *ant*."

2. Yet the word survived in the mouth of Lord Peter Whimsey in the Dorothy Sayers novels of the 1920s and 1930s, even though Dickens, writing in the 1860s, used it as a "low" dialect word.

III. Let's now turn to a set of words that illustrate issues of power and control, politics and paper.

A. When we look at a definition in a dictionary, we are looking at a narrative. As we'll see in a subsequent lecture, the makers of the OED borrowed the idea that words told stories from German philologists and dictionary makers of the 19th century. One famous German classicist said that every word should tell the *Lebensgeschichte* of a language—the "life history" of a language.

B. In addition to giving us a sequence in linear form of historical word use and word change, dictionaries also frequently offer narratives of how words came into the language. For example, at the end of the last lecture, we noted the OED's narratives for *protocol* and *quiz*.

C. Let's look at a specific word as an example of the historical narratives provided by the OED.

    1. The word *cheap* is a story of extension-in-lexis more than 2,000 years old, from the Germanic languages into English. The word is a product of the period of continental borrowing, the time before the Germanic tribes (and languages) split up, when many words for commerce, warfare, architecture, and social control were borrowed from Latin.

    2. All the modern Germanic languages have a word that comes from the Latin *caupo*, meaning "small merchant." In Modern German, *kaufen* is a verb meaning "to buy and sell"; a *Kaufmann* is a "merchant." The name of the city Copenhagen can be traced back to an older Norse word that meant "merchant's harbor or haven."

    3. In Old and Middle English, the word *cheap* underwent extension-in-lexis to refer to the thing bought or sold, the quality of the purchase. The result was such idioms as *good cheap*, meaning a good buy, and *dear cheap*, a seeming oxymoron meaning something scarce and expensive.

    4. Throughout London, there still exist place names and street names, such as Cheapside, that refer to market areas. As we saw in Shakespeare's Sonnet 87, the language of commercial exchange could also be applied to a love relationship.

5. In the 17th century, the word *cheap* took on its modern sense, that is, something that is inexpensive or easy to obtain and, thus, likely to be of low quality.

6. What we see in this narrative history of the extension-in-lexis of *cheap* is a history of the economy of the British Isles and the relationship between scarcity and value that came to control the market and credit economy.

D. The words *protocol*, *diploma*, and *collate* also illustrate changes in meaning from the specific to the general and pose problems for the lexicographer.

1. These three words all ultimately relate to pieces of paper.

   a. *Diploma*, for example, is a 16th- or 17th-century coinage from the Greek *diplos*, meaning "to fold over." A diploma is, quite simply, a folded piece of paper.

   b. In Medieval Latin, a *diploma* was a charter or a document, an important state paper folded over and sealed with wax. Thus, *diplomacy* became the practice of conducting state business through folded pieces of paper.

   c. It was not until the early 18th century that the word *diploma* was first used to refer to the documentation associated with a university degree.

   d. In this word, we see the transference of meaning from textual to political phenomena, that is, from the material of organization to the behavior surrounding that material.

2. The word *collate* comes from Latin and means simply "to compare or confer." In the 17th century, it acquired the meaning of bringing texts together to make certain kinds of comparisons.

3. In Greek, the *colophon* is similar to a title page, on which the scribe wrote his name and information about the document. The *proto-colophon* was what came before the colophon, the first sheet of a manuscript. From this, we get the word *protocol*, which like *diplomacy*, relates to the business of paper.

    a. Even today, the OED maintains the judgmental 19th-century definitions of *protocol* as a word that was not fully part of the English vocabulary.

    b. The most recent edition of the OED dates the earliest use of the word in its modern sense to 1952.

  E. Once again, we'll conclude with the word *quiz*. As we saw in the last lecture, the OED writes out the etymology of this word as a statement of linguistic politics.

IV. Dictionaries are not simply objective or empirical recorders of meaning. They are narrative documents imbued with the politics of nationhood and identity, concerned with describing—but invariably prescribing—language. Further, they are documents that are enmeshed in their own histories.

Reading:

J. A. H. Murray, et al., eds., *The Oxford English Dictionary*.

M. L. Samuels. *Linguistic Evolution with Special Reference to English* (from which material in this lecture is adapted).

Questions to Consider:

1. Define and give an example of polysemy and extension in lexis.

2. How do dictionaries reflect a hierarchy of meaning, and is this a problem?

Lecture Twenty-Three—Transcript
Dictionaries and Word Histories

What's a dictionary good for? In my previous lectures, I've illustrated the ways in which English dictionaries originated in the "hard word" lists of the 16th and 17th centuries, how they responded to the influx of new words and coinages into the English vocabulary—how in the figure of Samuel Johnson, the idea of the dictionary as a book for the home, for the individual, as keyed to aesthetic judgment, and as located in a view of language as mutable and transitory—how all of these things come together to bequeath to us the modern idioms and ideologies of dictionary-making.

I also suggested that when we look at modern dictionaries such as the *Oxford English Dictionary*, what we're also looking at is the legacy of these 18th-century lexicographers. In the work of William Lowth and Joseph Priestley, I illustrated the tensions between prescriptivism on the one hand and descriptivism on the other. Broadly speaking, I tried to illustrate how dictionaries invariable toe the line with great difficulty, between describing and prescribing usage.

What I would like to do in this lecture is look at some words and some aspects of change in meaning, in particular, to show what a dictionary is good for, or, to put it more precisely, how we can use a historical dictionary such as the *Oxford English Dictionary*—the OED—how we can use such a dictionary to give us access and insight into individual words and some principles, perhaps, of semantic change.

One of the things that I have resisted doing in the course of these lectures is asking and answering "why" questions. Why does language change? Why do words change meaning? Why did the Great Vowel Shift happen, and so on. Linguists, and historical linguists in particular, shy away from offering explanations for why particular changes happened. We can document them in great detail, but what the relationship is between social pressure or class involvement or the anatomy of the mouth or contact among languages and dialects, all of these, what the precise relationship is among them, is invariably doubtful and debatable.

What I would like to do, however, is suggest some "whys" for language change in this lecture, or to put it more precisely again, to provide some contexts for explaining how certain words change their meaning and perhaps therefore, look forward to the ways in which our own words might change their meaning in the future.

I'd like to begin with a set of principles that I've drawn from some recent works of linguistic theory and the history of language. One principle is what is called the relationship of ambiguity and limitation—that is, the argument that if a word or a form has two meanings so incompatible that they cause ambiguity, one of the meanings dies out, or, more rarely, the form itself becomes obsolete. Ambiguity and limitation, I think, have two sub-species, as it were. One of them is homonymy.

We all know what a homonym is. We all know that homonyms are two words which are pronounced identically, but which mean radically different things, like T-H-E-R-E and T-H-E-I-R—*there* and *their*. When I was a child growing up in Brooklyn, homonymy became for me a point of enormous tension because I, like so many children of my generation, was taught to distinguish with great precision between a word like *which* ("wh-") "which," the relative pronoun and *witch*, a sorceress (without the "h"). I was taught that the aspiration of the "wh" was different from the non-aspiration of the "w." But for me and for my peers, *which* and *witch* remained homonyms for life.

A vivid moment of personal embarrassment also remains for me that moment in second grade when we were all supposed to go around the room and come up with homonyms. In my best Brooklyn accent of the time, I reported that I had a pair of homonyms and it was *often*, and the teacher said, "What do you mean?" I said, "Well, *often*, I go to the store; and little *orphan* Annie." Clearly, these were not homonyms, but I'm offering this little tidbit to show you that homonymy remains both culturally and personally for many people an issue of contention.

For Old English speakers, homonymy may have also provoked change in language. An extreme example of homonym are the following set of words in Old English. The word *a*, which means *ever*; the word *ae*, which means *law*; the word *aeg*, which means *egg*; the word *ea*, which means *water*, the word *eoh*, which means *horse*; and the word *ieg*, which means *island*. If you see them spelled on the page and you pay attention to the precision of my pronunciation, you could argue, well, they probably aren't homonyms. But in everyday speech and certainly in casual conversation, the similarities of pronunciation may have been so great that in order to avoid ambiguity—that is, in order to limit the possible misunderstandings and misapprehensions of the word—different words came in, either from other languages, or from other dialects.

For example, the word *ae*, for *law*, disappears and is replaced by the word that eventually becomes *law*, that comes originally from Latin and the Romance languages. The word *aeg*, meaning *egg*, eventually disappears in its West Saxon or southern Middle English form and is replaced by the unambiguous Northern or Scandinavian form *egg*. You will remember Caxton's story of the mercers—that is, the London merchants who are trying to buy eggs in Kent— and go to the farmhouse, and they ask for eggs. And the wife says, "I speak no French." They are looking for *eyre—eyren*.

Here, the issue is that perhaps a form from another regional dialect comes in in order to disambiguate homonymy and make possible the fewest number of confusions. This is one potential explanation for change in language. We've seen polysemy previously—that is, where one word has several meanings. Some of these meanings can overlap over time. Let me give you some examples of polysemy to show how using the resources of a historical dictionary—like the *Oxford English Dictionary*—can help us understand something of change in meaning in an individual word.

The word I'm going to focus on is *uncouth*. *Uncouth* means *not couth*. *Couth* comes from the Germanic root meaning *known*, or being aware of something. Something that in Old English was "uncouth" was something that was simply unknown or unfamiliar, or strange. This form survives in written and spoken English until the middle of the 17th century. Gradually, the word came to describe things that were not simply unknown, but were strange or unpleasant because they were unknown. This meaning originates probably at the end of the 14th century, and can still be found in some regional uses today.

Uncomely, awkward, and *clumsy* is another set of definitions that the OED gives, and this version probably begins in its earliest citation at the beginning of the 16th century. In the middle of the 16th century, if you were *uncouth,* you were rough and rugged; and by the end of the 17th century, only by the end of the 17th century, does the word *uncouth* mean *uncultured* in this modern way.

What I want to show in this kind of narrative is the way in which you have a word of several meanings overlapping over time, and as we've seen throughout these lectures, the way in which change in meaning can move from a particular condition to a description grounded in that condition. Something that is unknown becomes something that is alien, strange, weird, rugged, rough, uncultured. What we have here is the true etymology of *uncouth.* What we do not have is the bogus, or folk etymology of *uncouth.* The idea that *uncouth* means now *uncultured* and therefore that there must be a root in uncouth without the "un"—*couth,* where *couth* takes on this imagined nominal status, as in a phrase like, "He's got no couth." That is imaginary; it is completely a-historical. I wonder if eventually the word will change and that future lexicographers will record the meaning of a word *"couth"* as emerging in the late 20th and early 21st centuries to mean *propriety, ability, culture, knowledge, skill*—to have *couth.*

So these are examples of homonymy and polysemy, and they are the sub-species of ambiguity and limitation. Another way in which words change their meaning is through what is called "extension in lexis," and I've used this term before. Extension in lexis is where metaphorical meanings or figurative senses take over from older technical or literal meanings. Let me give you some examples, also drawn from the information available in the *Oxford English Dictionary.*

The verb *clog,* originally meant *to fasten wood* to something, and that first appears at the end of the 14th century. It's only by the beginning of the 16th century that the verb *clog* means *to encumber by adhesion.* So you can see here extension in lexis—that is, a gradual figurative sense from something very, very specific. So now when pipes get clogged or something like that, there's nothing about wood or fastening in it, it's simply an issue of encumbrance.

The verb *to clasp* means *to fasten* in Middle English; it means *to enfold* by early Modern English, and by the end of the 16th century, it means *to grip* with the hand. *Brazen* is a beautiful word and it's another word that illustrates extension in lexis. *Brazen* simply means *of brass*—brass: brazen. This is its Old English and Middle English meaning. If something was made of brass, it was invariably made in order to pass for something else that looked like brass, and that is gold. Renaissance writers write frequently of the difference between the golden age of the past and what they called "this brazen world."—that is, a world not *brazen* in the sense of being impudent, but of being made of brass rather than of gold.

To be brassy or to be *brazen* gradually took on this social sense, as if being brazen was to try to make your brass pass for true gold. So it's only by the end of the 16th century that brazen constitutes a category of social behavior rather than a quality of metallurgy.

To bristle is *to stand up stiff*, like the bristles of a brush. But by the middle of the 16th century, it means to *become indignant*—that is, you metaphorically bristle. I'll give you one more example. *To broil* is to burn in Middle English, and by the time of Shakespeare, it is *to get angry*. What I'm illustrating here through these particular examples are the ways in which words change meaning, by taking on figurative or metaphorical meanings that eventually displace the older technical meaning.

As I've repeatedly said, this is an important problem in semantic change. Especially when you organize a dictionary as Samuel Johnson did. Johnson recognized it in the making of his dictionary. So what he did was he organized the definitions so that the older, primary, or non-metaphorical meaning came first even if that meaning was no longer current. This is a very important principle of lexicography—that is, that in this tradition of lexicography, which is followed by the *Oxford English Dictionary*, and by several other modern dictionaries, you are out to record not the word definitions in order of popularity or familiarity. You are out to record the word definitions historically where the hierarchization, the principle of hierarchy, is from the literal to the figurative.

Lexicography, therefore, creates the impression of hierarchies of meaning, even when those hierarchies may not actually reflect the uses of the time. So when we look at a dictionary, we're looking at a history of words told through the history of semantic change. These tiers of meaning can be both literal and figurative tiers, and tiers of class.

I mentioned in my previous lecture the case of *ain't* in the 18th century. It was used by polite society, frequently in the form of *ant*, and the OED considers *ain't*, "a later and more literate form of *ant*." Yet, as I mentioned, it survived in the mouth of Lord Peter Wimsey in the Dorothy Sayers novels of the '20s and '30s, even though Charles Dickens, writing in the 1860s marked it as a "low" dialect word.

So these matters infuse the definitions in the dictionary, and what I'd like to do now is build on some observations at the close of my previous lecture to look at a set of words where we can see issues in power and control, politics and paper.

When we look at a definition in a dictionary, what we're looking at are narratives. This is a very important point—that is, dictionaries are narrative phenomena. They're narrative phenomena in several ways. First, because the historical organization of a dictionary tells a story, every word should tell a story. And in my subsequent lecture, I'm going to call attention to the way in which the makers of the *Oxford English Dictionary* explicitly made clear that words told stories. They borrowed this idea from the Germanic philologists and dictionary-makers of the 19th century, where, in the words of one famous German classicist, every word should tell, what he called, the *Lebensgeschichte* of a language—that is, the life history of a language.

Dictionaries are narrative because they record a sequence in linear form of historical word use and word change. Dictionaries are also narrative because very often the definitions or the head notes of the explanations tell stories of how words came into the language.

At the close of my previous lecture, I hinted at some ways in which the OED offers narratives for a couple of words—in particular, *protocol* and *quiz*—and at the end of this lecture, I'm going to return to those in some greater detail.

Let's look at a couple of words to see what's going on in historical narrative. Some of these words I've talked about in the course of my lectures, and now I want to review some of them systematically to go through these histories. One of the most compelling words in such a history is the word *cheap*. The word *cheap* is a story of extension in lexis more than 2,000 years old, from the Germanic languages into English. This is a word that is the product of a period of continental borrowing.

You'll remember in my lectures on the Germanic languages, the period of continental borrowing was that period before the Germanic languages split up, before the Angles and the Saxons and the Jutes came to the British Isles, when the Germanic peoples came in contact with the Latin of the Roman Empire. Many of the words that were borrowed from Latin at that time were words for commerce, and warfare, and architecture, and social control. So all of the Germanic languages will have these words in their modern forms, and the word *cheap* comes from the Latin word *caupo*, which originally meant a small merchant.

In German, Modern German, it is *kaufen*, the verb meaning to buy and often to sell as well. A *Kaufmann* is a merchant. You have, as I've mentioned before, the name Copenhagen, the city, which goes back to an older Norse word *Kaupmannhofen*—that is, the haven, or the harbor for the *Kaupmann*—for the person involved in buying and selling—that is, the merchant's haven. In the course of Old and Middle English, the word *cheap* extends its lexis beyond simply buying and selling to refer to the thing itself, or to the quality of the purchase. So you have idioms like good cheap, which refers to a low price, or a good buy.

This develops in the Middle English period. You have a phrase like "dear cheap," which may seem to us like an oxymoron, or a contradiction. Here the phrase means something expensive, where there is a dearth or scarcity of the product.

In place names and street names, still in London today, there is Cheapside and East Cheap. These names go back to a time when these areas were the market or the mercantile places of congregation. In such places as Cheapside, where you might get *good cheap*, you might also find things that were *cheap* or dear. The distinction between something *cheap* and something dear does not appear in the *Oxford English Dictionary* until the beginning of the 16th century.

We saw in Shakespeare's Sonnet 87 how the language of commercial exchange can inform the language of love, and how a love relationship could be expressed in terms of, if you like, purchase or investment.

What is, in effect, the *cheap* of love? By the 17th century, the word takes on its modern senses—that is, something which is inexpensive or easy to obtain, and therefore something which is most likely of low quality. What we see in the narrative history of the extension in lexis in a word like *cheap* is a history of the economy of the British Isles and the relationship between scarcity and value that, by the 16th and 17th century, controls the market and credit economy.

There is a clutch of words that fascinate me, that also illustrate changes in meaning from the specific to the general and that also pose problems for the lexicographer. I talked a little bit about *protocol*, and I want to bring into that discussion now two other words: *diploma* and *collate*. *Protocol, diploma,* and *collate* are all words that are ultimately about pieces of paper. Take a word like *diploma*. *Diploma* is a coinage in the 16th and 17th centuries from Greek—that is, scholars made up the word from a Greek word meaning to fold over—*diplos*. A *diploma* is, quite simply, a folded piece of paper.

In medieval Latin, *diploma* was a charter or a document. Important state papers, because they were private or because they were secret, would be folded over and they would be sealed with wax. So *diplomatics* became the study of folded pieces of paper. *Diplomacy* was the practice of conducting state business through folded pieces of paper. A *diploma* was something that granted you authority. If you were *diplomatic* about something, you would write it on a piece of paper and fold it.

At this point, I'm being figurative and playful with the etymology, but this etymology of the folded piece of paper is still a living meaning for the 18th century. It's not until the early 18th century that the word *diploma* is first used to refer to something that you get when you get a university degree. *Diplomatics*, therefore, is a transference of meaning from textual to political phenomena—that is, from the material of organization to the behavior around that material.

Let me look at another word about paper, and that's the word *collate*. The word *collate* comes from the Latin, and in Latin, you have the verbs. There are certain kinds of verbs in Latin whose principal parts are made up of other parts of other verbs. In the case of the verb *to confer*—*confere, confero* (to make two things come together, or to compare them)—the participial form of *confere* is *collatus*. So to *collate* was really just to compare or simply to confer things.

It really isn't until the 17th century that the word *collate* comes to mean to bring texts together in order to make certain kinds of comparisons. *Colophon*, in Greek, is the part of a document that the scribe has written his name, or the title, or the information about that document. We still use that word to some extent today.

The thing that came before the colophon was, in Greek, the *proto-colophon*—the thing before. So *protocol* comes from a Greek set of terms to mean the first sheet or the roll of papyrus, or the first sheet in a manuscript. So the business of protocol, like the business of diplomatics, was the business of paper.

In my previous lecture, I noted how the *Oxford English Dictionary*, even to this day, maintains and still reproduces the older judgmental 19th-century definitions of *protocol* as a word which was not fully part of the English vocabulary, but rather came from the formulary of etiquette in France, or that came from the language of the legal vocabulary of Latin or French. If we delve deeper into *protocol*, we see other forms of alienation. This is the kind of stuff that I'm suggesting to you that you can do with a great historical dictionary: read behind the definitions.

Here, and I pick almost at random from the several columns of definition of *protocol*:

> In the parts of the United States acquired from Mexico, the name is used for the original record of a grant, transfer, etc. of land; under the Spanish law this was an entry made in the book by the official recorder of such transactions.

Once again, we have a definition that is privileged. This appears very early in the narrative. This definition privileges the alien or unusual quality of the word *protocol*. Now as I mentioned, the *Oxford English Dictionary* was begun in the late 19th and completed in the early 20th century, and it's been constantly updated. In the most recent edition of the OED, it's not until the very end that you get the modern expected use.

> In extended and general uses, any code of conventional or proper conduct, formerly correct behavior.

The earliest citation for this use that the OED gives is 1952. What we're looking at is a narrative. What we're looking at is a story of pieces of paper that become modes of behavior. I talked too, about *quiz* at the end of my last lecture. Once again, I will conclude with *quiz*, a word of dubious origin. As I showed, the OED has problems with the etymology, where it writes out that etymology as a statement of linguistic politics. It is a word of the theater; it is perhaps a word of Irish origin, from the theater manager Daly of Dublin. Whatever is at stake here, the various forms of *quiz*, meaning a test, or meaning the verb to inquire, whatever is going on here, we see an etymology that challenges the lexicographical resources of the OED.

To wrap up this particular lecture and look forward to the next, we need to recognize that dictionaries are not simply objective or empirical recorders of meaning. They are narrative documents imbued with the politics of nationhood and identity; concerned very much with describing, but invariably prescribing, or regulating language; and furthermore, they are documents and they are volumes that are enmeshed in their own history.

I'll begin my next lecture with the beginnings of the *Oxford English Dictionary*, and then move through to conclude this second block of lectures in this series with some attitudes towards English and national and cultural identity toward the close of the 20th and the beginning of the 21st centuries.

Lecture Twenty-Four
Values, Words, and Modernity

Scope:

How do we bear the legacy of earlier approaches to the study and teaching of English? In dictionaries, such as the OED; in handbooks, such as *Fowler's Modern English Usage*; and in contemporary debates on language use, we may see the same terms and problems as we saw in the age of Samuel Johnson. This lecture illustrates not only how we may place these arguments in historical contexts but also how we may recognize the immense impact of these earlier discussions.

Outline

I. The OED remains one of the great monuments of historical lexicography, and its own history is, in many ways, the history of the discipline of historical linguistics and of many political, economic, and institutional developments of England in the 19th and 20th centuries. In this lecture, we'll explore the origins of the OED and learn something about its makers; we'll also look at some of the legacies of the OED in representative writers of the 20th century on language use and its arbitration.

II. The origins of the OED can be found in the philological inquiries of mid-19th-century England.

    A. In the late 18th and early 19th centuries, inquiries into language shifted from the philosophical and metaphysical to the empirical and the historical. By the middle of the 19th century, the discipline of philology became something of a historical science on a par with geology, anatomy, and biology.

        1. The Philological Society was founded in 1842, in London, to study the history of languages and institutionalize the work in Indo-European and comparative philology that was coming to dominate language study in Europe by the mid-19th century.

        2. By this time, scholars of language were increasingly located in schools and universities. This marks a shift

from 18th-century language study, which tended to be pursued by amateurs (exemplified by the character Mr. Casaubon from George Eliot's novel *Middlemarch*), journalists, poets, and professional men of letters (such as Samuel Johnson).

3. In 1864, the Early English Text Society (EETS), which still exists today, was founded to recover, edit, and publish editions of early English writings. These editions were used as source materials for the OED.

B. Historical linguistics was pressed into the service of nationalist ideologies in the 19th century. To paraphrase Karl von Clausewitz's famous statement about war, philology was politics by other means.

1. Competing scholars in the various European and classical languages—English, German, French, Italian, and others—made claims for the legitimacy and value of national vernaculars in a larger European context.

2. A fascinating figure in this debate was Max Müller (1823–1900), the ultimate arbiter of language in mid-19th-century England.

3. Müller's work raised questions about the power of language to confer identity on human beings and values in society. He was fascinated with mythology, in particular by the idea of a sun god in Indo-European mythology.

4. Much of Müller's work has come in for criticism by later linguists, but it is interesting in its investment of words with narrative meaning. As he put it, "Words mean more than they have ever meant before." Once one knows the etymology of a word, it acquires another layer of meaning.

5. What, we might ask, does a word refer to? Does the meaning of a word lie in its representational ability or in its history over time? This is one of the most philosophically profound issues in Victorian philology—the way in which words come to refer more to their own histories than to their objective status in the world.

C. In 1857, the Philological Society proposed to create a new English dictionary to establish English etymology and usage on a firm "scientific" basis.

   1. The original editors were Herbert Coleridge and Richard Trench. Trench claimed a "true idea" of the dictionary, which he said should be "an inventory of the language." The job of the dictionary maker was not to hierarchize words—not to keep some out and privilege others—but to make an account of language.

   2. Thus, the lexicographer was no longer Samuel Johnson's "harmless drudge" but a historian of language and of a people, as well as a kind of overseer in the great factory of language.

   3. In the 1870s, when Sir James A. H. Murray was appointed general editor of the OED, he set up the Scriptorium, indeed, a word factory. In the words of the modern historian and critic of the OED Hans Aarsleff, the dictionary of a language, in this case the OED, became "an historical monument, the history of a nation contemplated from one point of view."

III. The OED provides not only lexicographical models but social and, indeed, moral models, as well. In the remainder of this lecture, we'll look at selected statements by writers and editors that have been highly influential in the 20th century and that represent earlier debates generated by 19th-century linguistic science and lexicography.

   A. Some of the main themes in these statements include the following:

   1. The relationship between language and society: Is language the reflection of social behavior? What is the relationship between linguistic propriety and social propriety? How is the study of the history of language the study of the history of the people?

   2. The role of authority and education in articulating the relationship between language and society: Whose job is it to study language and to teach it? Is the institution of language study to be compared, as Johnson did, to the institution of imperial control? Is it to be compared with a factory or a university seminary?

3. The relationship between style and grammar: Where do we draw the line between grammatical correctness and stylistic choice?

4. The relationship between description and prescription: What is the goal of linguistic study—to describe behavior or to prescribe standards? And how does a writer on language exemplify language itself?

B. In Henry Fowler's article on grammar from *Modern English Usage*, we can hear the key idioms of the debates that we have seen at work from the beginning of this course: Does the history of English reflect a move from an inflected to uninflected language? Is that history still in process? Is that history moving toward a goal?

1. Consider Fowler's aesthetic vocabulary, which includes such phrases as "ease and grace," "clearly and agreeably," and the equation of good grammar with "good manners."

2. Like others before him, he seems to phrase the question of grammaticality as a question of sociability. For Fowler, aesthetic judgment is the primary criterion of assessment of linguistic performance.

C. In the introduction to *Webster's New World Dictionary of the American Language* (9th ed.), entitled "Language and the Dictionary," we note again the discussion of prescriptivism versus descriptivism.

1. We also hear the organic metaphors of the 18th century and Samuel Johnson: "A good dictionary can promote order in inevitable growth." Here, a "good" dictionary performs a service for society.

2. Fowler, too, discusses the "good work" a dictionary can perform in helping to purge the language of its sins, in this instance, case inflections. The role of the dictionary is akin to that of a pastor.

D. In a 1972 article in the journal *The American Scholar*, Douglas Bush of Harvard University asserts that change in language should be "inaugurated from above by the masters of language..., not from below." A kind of modern Alexander Gil, Bush goes beyond linguistic prescriptivism to embrace social prescriptivism.

E. We close with a famous excerpt from George Orwell's "Politics and the English Language," in which he tells us that euphemism is not just a form of politeness, but it can also be used to serve the ends of political deceit.

F. Our next set of lectures will look at these discussions in the American trajectory, beginning with colonial expansion and moving on to our present time.

Reading:

Hans Aarsleff, *The Study of Language in England, 1780–1860.*

Linda Dowling, "Victorian Oxford and the Science of Language."

Linda Mugglestone, *Lost for Words: The Hidden History of the OED.*

K. M. Elisabeth Murray, *Caught in the Web of Words: James A. H. Murray and the Oxford English Dictionary.*

Questions to Consider:

1. What historical developments of the 19th century led to the creation of the *Oxford English Dictionary*?

2. According to Orwell, why are polysyllabic words more likely to deceive than short, simple ones? Do you agree?

Lecture Twenty-Four—Transcript
Values, Words, and Modernity

The *Oxford English Dictionary* remains one of the great monuments of historical lexicography. In its collaborative production from the 1880s to the 1920s, in its many supplements, and now in its online version, it bears eloquent testimony to the researches and resources of the many who put it all together.

The OED began with a group of amateurs and it continued through its early life by drawing on volunteers to provide slips of paper with representative quotations of literature and words, both common and uncommon. The history of the *Oxford English Dictionary* is in many ways the history not just of the English language, but the history of the discipline of historical linguistics, and also the history of so many of the political, economic, and institutional developments of England in the 19th and the 20th century. It might not be too much to say that, together with the King James Bible, the *Oxford English Dictionary* is the single greatest collaborative effort in the history of the English language.

In this lecture, I want to talk a little bit about the origins of the *Oxford English Dictionary*, say a few things about the people who made it, and also look at some of the legacies of the OED in some representative writers of the 20th century on language use and its arbitration.

The origins of the OED are to be found in the philological inquiries of mid-19th-century England. You'll remember from my earlier lectures on Indo-European, how the late-18th- and early-19th-century inquirers into language shifted the study of language from something that was philosophical and metaphysical on the one hand, to something that was empirical and historical on the other. The discipline of philology, by the middle of the 19th century, became something of an historical science, it was believed, on a par with the history of the earth itself—with geology; with historical and comparative anatomy; with biology; and then after Darwin, with evolutionary biology.

The Philological Society culminated several decades of interest among learned amateurs in England, and it was founded in 1842 in London for the purpose of studying the history of languages. It institutionalized, if you like, the work in Indo-European and comparative philology which was coming to dominate language study in Europe by the mid-19th century.

Let me just pause for a little bit and say something about this world of the philological in the 19th century. Scholars of language by the mid-19th century came increasingly to be located in schools and universities. During the 18th century and before, people who studied language were largely learned amateurs. They were, if you like, country-house philologists. They were journalists, poets, or they were people like Samuel Johnson, who was a professional man of letters, who—even though he had training and eventually was to receive an honorary doctorate—was not someone who spent his life in a university.

This is beginning to change in the first decades of the 19th century. It seems to me that for those of you more familiar with, let's say, the history of English literature than with the history of the English language, that a very good example of somebody on the cusp of this change is the figure of Mr. Casaubon from George Eliot's novel *Middlemarch*. This novel, though published in 1870 and '71, is set in the period from 1828 to 1830. It is precisely at this moment of transition Mr. Casaubon claims to have discovered a key to all mythologies.

He is an amateur. He is a member of the church. He is a pedant. And Mr. Casaubon reacts strongly when characters in the novel do not understand, or mock what he's doing, and one of the characters, Will Ladislaw explains that, "The Germans have figured this all out. The Germans have done this." What he's referring to by "the Germans" is he's referring to the Indo-European philologists—people like Franz Bopp and the Brothers Grimm, who in the early 19th century codified the rules and the laws of Indo-European; were looking at the languages; and, in effect, provided the key to all mythologies, which in some sense, was historical comparative philology rather than country-house, amateur antiquarianism.

This is, if you like, a fictional representation of the historical moment in the 19th century when scholarship moves from the amateur to the professional. So what we have in the case of the Philological Society is another move from the amateurism of the learned to the gradual ensconcing of the professional in the university. So the Philological

Society's foundation in 1842 was keyed to the production of a new English dictionary. As I mentioned in a previous lecture, the impress of Samuel Johnson's *Dictionary* of 1755 was so profound that when the idea of another English dictionary was proposed, it was to be the *New* English dictionary because Johnson's was the Old.

In order to provide texts—accurate, historical texts for this new English dictionary—another society had to be founded. In 1864, a society called the Early English Text Society was founded to recover, edit, and publish editions of early English writings. These editions came to be used as source materials for the OED. It is an interesting fact of British intellectual and academic life that the EETS, as it is called, is still going strong today, and a couple of volumes are being published still year by year to this day—testimony to the survival in many ways of 19th-century historical philology and editorial method.

What are the larger goals of this historical philological project? Historical linguistics came to be pressed into the service of the nationalist ideologies of the 19th century. Karl von Clausewitz has a very famous statement, which is very often paraphrased—indeed parodied—that "war is politics by other means."

I would suggest that for the 19th century, philology was politics by other means—that is, that by looking at the histories of the languages—English, German, French, Italian, the various European and the classical languages—competing scholars throughout Europe made claims for the legitimacy of national vernaculars and, furthermore, for the relative value of those national vernaculars in a larger European context.

One of the most fascinating figures of this history is a man named Max Müller who lived from 1823 to 1900. And while he was German in birth and training, he came to spend the bulk of his professional career at Oxford University. In mid-19th-century England, Max Müller was the arbiter of language. There's a story going around among linguists and historians—perhaps it's true, perhaps it's apocryphal—that any letter addressed to the Professor of Language at Oxford—no name, no post code, nothing else—would go immediately to Max Müller. It was the linguistic equivalent of writing to Santa Claus, care of the North Pole.

Müller's work is fascinating largely because what he tried to do was raise questions about the power of human language to confer identity on human beings and values in society. Among his fascinations were, if you want to phrase it in this Casaubonian term, "a key to all mythologies." Müller was fascinated by mythology and he was fascinated by the idea of the sun god in Indo-European mythology.

Much of Müller's work has come in for criticism by later linguists, but what is interesting about it is the way in which he invested words with narrative meaning. This goes back to a point I was making earlier. Dictionaries tell stories. Well, now words tell stories, and one of Müller's most famous and notable quotations in many of his works was the idea, as he put it, that "words mean more than they have ever meant before."

What does that mean? Part of what it means is that once you know the etymology of a word, once you know its transformation over time, then it's hard to use that word in the same way again, as you had before. I've given you some etymologies: *protocol, colophon, quiz, diploma, cheap, silly, uncouth*. Now, what I hope is that these words mean more to you than they have ever meant before. You are aware of their linguistic history, and whether or not you use those words in their linguistically historical context, there is another layer of meaning to them.

What Müller recognized was that the discipline of historical philology gave each word a larger resonance and larger context. And this contributed to a larger mid-19th century or, if you like, Victorian attitude towards language. What the Victorians recognized was that in many ways, words really did mean more than they had meant before, and that the stories of words became what words were about.

This is an interesting, if you like, almost philosophical problem. What does a word refer to? In other words, does the meaning of a word lie in its representational ability? That is, if I say the word *door*, does the meaning of that word hinge on the thing on the hinges? If by contrast I say the word *door* and the first thing I think of is the history of the word *door*, and its cognates in the Germanic languages, and the idea of the door or the doorway, and the notion of the portal in Indo-European. If I play this whole thing out in my head, then at a certain level, what the word *door* refers to is not primarily the object in the room, but the history of the word over time.

This is, it seems to me, one of the most philosophically profound things about Victorian philology—the way in which words come to refer more to their history than to their objective status in the world. So the idea that words meant more than they ever meant before motivated the founding of the Philological Society, and the idea of a new English dictionary. So in 1857, the Philological Society proposed a new English dictionary as a way of establishing English etymology and usage on what they called a firm, scientific basis.

The original editors were a man named Herbert Coleridge and Richard Trench. Both of them wrote in prefaces, in letters, and in essays, statements about their goals for this dictionary. Richard Trench, the original editor of the OED, claimed a true idea of the dictionary. What he said is that a dictionary should be an inventory of the language. So the idea here was that the job of the dictionary-maker was not to hierarchize words—not to keep some out and privilege some in—the idea was to inventory. That word *inventory* carries with it a profound economic and social resonance for the mid-19th century.

The lexicographer is a historian of language, a historian of a people, but the lexicographer is, if you like, the overseer in the great factory of language. You are inventorying your words. You are going, in effect, into the storehouse of words. A lexicographer is no longer Samuel Johnson's harmless drudge; a lexicographer is an industrial person—a person of industry; a person of industriousness.

In the 1870s, when Sir James A. H. Murray was appointed the new overseer Editor of the *Oxford English Dictionary*, he set up what was called the Scriptorium—the great factory. Indeed, he called it a factory. He called it a word factory, and it was full of pigeonholes and it was full of great walls and rooms, and it was an industry of words. So in the words of the great modern historian and critic of the OED, Hans Aarsleff, the dictionary of a language, in this case the OED, became an historical monument—the history of a nation contemplated from one point of view. In other words, it was as much a monument as any of the great edifices of industry that were being built in the 19th century.

The OED provides not only lexicographical models, but social and moral ones as well. What I would like to do in the remainder of this lecture is look at some selected statements by writers and editors that have been highly influential in the 20th century, and that represent earlier debates generated by the kind of linguistic inquiries of the 18th century and the linguistic science of the 19th century.

I want to summarize ahead of time what some of my key points will be, drawing on this arc of historical progression. In other words— from Johnson through the makers of the OED—this notion, first, of a relationship between language and society. Is language the reflection of social behavior? What is the relationship between linguistic propriety and social propriety, and how is the study of the history of language the study of the history of the people? All of these questions and issues are raised in the traditions of lexicography from Johnson to the OED, and all of them can be found at levels of detail in the definitions of words and the quotations illustrating those definitions.

Next, the question of the role of authority in education in articulating the relationship between language and society. In other words, whose job is it to study language and to teach it? Is it the job of the enlightened amateur? Is it the job of the journalist? Is it the job of the degree-holding professional? Is the institution of language study to be compared to, as Johnson did, the institution of imperial control, where Johnson's *Dictionary* becomes, in effect, like an act of conquest? Is it to be compared to a kind of Victorian industry or factory? Is it to be compared with a university seminar?

One of the central questions adjudicated by such arbiters of language is: when do you draw the line between style and grammar? In other words, I can speak perfectly grammatically, but I may at times speak in a way that is idiosyncratic and that may be by style. Further, one may elect to speak ungrammatically for purposes of stylistic enhancement. Where do we draw the line between grammatical correctness on the one hand and stylistic choice on the other?

These arbiters also tried to adjudicate the relationship between description and prescription—linguistic behavior on the one hand, linguistic standards on the other. One of the ways in which they did this was by becoming models of style in their own right. One of the things I've tried to stress throughout this course is that we read writers on language not simply for what they say, but how they say it. How does a writer on language exemplify language itself?

I turn now to four extended quotations to illustrate the ways in which writing on language is a performance of language, and how the issues of grammar and style, prescription, description, institution and industry, dictionary and definition, come together to grant us insight, but at times impediment, into our understanding of the English language.

My first quotation is from none other than the great Henry Fowler, who is the author of *Modern English Usage*. He's writing in the 1920s. Here is a selection from his article on grammar.

> We took a long time to realize that there is not much sense in trying to apply the rules of a dead synthetic language [by which Fowler means Latin], to a living analytical one. Perhaps we have not yet quite abandoned the attempt. It is for instance, despite the grammarians, not thanks to them, that over the centuries, our language has won ease and grace by getting rid of almost all its case inflections. Some day perhaps this good work will be complete and we shall no longer be faced with the sometimes puzzling task of choosing between *who* and *whom*. But it is going too far if we give the word *grammar* its proper meaning to say, as Orwell said, that "grammar is of no importance so long as we make our meaning plain." What are generally recognized for the time being as its conventions, must be followed by those who would write clearly and agreeably, and its elements must be taught in the schools if only as a code of good manners.

This is a remarkable quotation, and what's remarkable about it is the way I think you can still hear the key idioms of the debates that we have seen at work, really, from the beginning of this course—that is, what is English? Is English an inflected or an uninflected language? Is the history of English from one that was inflected to one that was uninflected? Is that history still in process? Is that history moving towards a goal—in other words, complete lack of grammatical inflection, where we will no longer distinguish between *who* and *whom*?

Is this a good thing? Furthermore, what are the institutions that will teach and arbitrate? Look at Fowler's aesthetic vocabulary. This goes back to Johnson and even before. The way in which he uses a phrase like "ease and grace." This is in so many ways a profoundly 18th-century kind of phrase. Or, the way in which he talks about writing "clearly and agreeably." Or, the very way in which an essay on grammar ends with a statement about good manners—that the elements of grammar, he says, "must be taught in the schools if only as a code of good manners."

Recall Fanny Burney on propriety. Recall the way in which the concept of propriety moved from a grammatical to a social concept. What I think Fowler is doing here is he is recapitulating the central lines of debate—that is, the question of grammaticality as a question of sociability; the question of aesthetic judgment as your primary criterion of assessment; and, furthermore, the need to maintain a level of rule-governed behavior in linguistic performance if only, as he says, "as a code of good manners."

Fowler's *Modern English Usage* has become a Bible for many, just as dictionaries have become Bibles of many. One of the most popular of the modern American dictionaries is *Webster's New World Dictionary of the American Language*. I'm going to quote from the Introduction to the ninth edition. This is called "Language and the Dictionary." I'm going to quote a paragraph from it. It reads as follows:

> Language rests upon use. Anything used long enough by enough people will become standard. A good dictionary can promote order in inevitable growth. It will also promote stability in the language by preserving evidence of the past, but it should not be treated mainly as a means to ensure linguistic atrophy.

By this point, you should know what to listen for, and what you listen for is the discussion between prescriptivism versus descriptivism. At one level, they're saying language is something that changes, and if enough people use a phrase, it will become standard. If enough people say things like, "He has no couth," whether or not it is historically accurate, will that become a standard? Will *couth*, in some sense, take on a new meaning?

We see once again the old, organic metaphors of the 18th century and of Samuel Johnson—promoting order and inevitable growth as if a dictionary was kind of like an English country gardener—letting things not run too wildly, but carefully trimming the hedges of language; promoting stability, as if the dictionary now was a political as well as a linguistic tool; preserving evidence, as if the dictionary was something like a scientist keeping specimens in jars of formaldehyde. Yet, language is a living thing and the organs of language should not be left, as the dictionary says, to atrophy.

Look also at the word "*good*"—a *good* dictionary. What is the difference between a good dictionary and a bad dictionary? A good dictionary, well, according to my 15-year-old son, a good dictionary is a dictionary that has all the dirty words in it. According to *Webster's New World Dictionary*, a good dictionary is one that promotes "order in inevitable growth." So the mark of a dictionary is not how many words it has in it; a mark of a dictionary is not whether it gives you good definitions or whether it enables your prurience as a reader; a good dictionary is something that performs a good service to society.

Go back to Fowler's quote and look at the way he uses the word *good*. When he's talking about how we will eventually get rid of all these case inflections, he says, "Some day, perhaps, this good work will be complete." The phrase "good work" must resonate with a kind of pastoral care—as if the good work of the dictionary, or like the good works of a pastor, or the good works that will get us into heaven—the phrase "good work" cannot but recall a moral and a religious activity. Now the good work will be to purge the language of its sins.

In 1972, Douglas Bush of Harvard University, one of the leading and perhaps self-appointed arbiters of literary and linguistic taste in the United States, wrote an essay in which he said,

> We know that language is always changing and growing, but acceptance of the perpetual process does not or should not mean blind surrender to the momentum or inertia of slovenly and tasteless ignorance and insensitivity. Ideally, changes should be inaugurated from above by the masters of language as they have often been, not from below. From the Greeks, notably Plato, and Romans onward, many men of

goodwill have been concerned about the use and abuse of language, and they did what they could to curb barbarism and foster taste, discipline, and integrity.

I'm just old enough to remember college in 1972, and I can tell you that in 1972, I and my compeers were slovenly, tasteless, and ignorant. We were insensitive to the masters of language and the last thing we wanted was change to be inaugurated from above. Douglas Bush writing from Harvard in 1972 is, in the end, writing less about language than he is writing about social and institutional upheaval. His terms veritably bristle with the language of political control.

Bush's notion, if you like, goes beyond linguistic prescriptivism to embrace social prescriptivism. We can see here Bush as a kind of modern Alexander Gil or William Lowth who raises the notion of propriety, and the origin of language change as a matter to be arbitrated rather than to be described.

Finally, I conclude with George Orwell, whose famous essay of the late-1940s "Politics and the English Language," has become a touchstone for any discussion of the history of English and its usage. In the course of this long quotation that I'm going to read, Orwell contrasts the Anglo-Saxon vocabulary with an imported Latinate diction. He signals that euphemism is not just a form of politeness, but it can be used to serve the ends of political deceit. Orwell's quotation is, of course, one of the most Orwellian things he ever wrote.

> In our time, political speech and writing are largely the defense of the indefensible. Things like the continuance of British rule in India, the Russian purges and deportations, the dropping of the atom bombs on Japan, can indeed be defended, but only by arguments which are too brutal for most people to face, and which do not square with the professed aims of the political parties. Thus political language has to consist largely of euphemism, question-begging and sheer cloudy vagueness. Defenseless villages are bombarded from the air, the inhabitants driven out into the countryside, the cattle machine-gunned, the huts set on fire with incendiary bullets: this is called "pacification." Millions of peasants are robbed of their farms and sent trudging along the roads with no more than they can carry:

this is called "transfer of population" or "rectification of frontiers." People are imprisoned for years without trial, or shot in the back of the neck or sent to die of scurvy in Arctic lumber camps: this is called "elimination of unreliable elements." Such phraseology is needed if one wants to name things without calling up mental pictures of them.

Orwell's quotation has been used so many times over the last 60 years, whether it was for the Stalinist purges or for the war in Korea, or for Vietnam, or for the conditions at the close of the 20th and the beginning of the 21st century, that I will not belabor the obvious resonances. What I simply want to call attention to is this: the way in which Orwell, like all the writers I have read to you, is a master of style. The way in which, like Chaucer, like Milton, like Shakespeare, he can juxtapose phrases of Old English origin with phrases of Romance or Latinate importation.

Euphemism, question-begging, sheer cloudy vagueness. An apposition that enacts the very claims it makes. How can something be both *sheer* and *cloudy* at the same time? The way in which he shows us that rewriting the present invariably leads us into the polysyllables of the Latinate. As we saw for Geoffrey Chaucer, as we saw for the trilingual culture of medieval England, the importation of a new society was the importation of a new world—*Castelas he let wyrcean*—that William the Conqueror built castles, a new thing and a new word.

I conclude with Orwell as a retrospective on the way in which the history of English has been a tension not just between prescription and description, but a tension between what we believe to be the native and the imported.

In the next set of lectures, the final third of this course, I'm going to look at these discussions in the American trajectory, beginning with colonial expansion and moving on to our present time.

Timeline

B.C.

4th–3rd millennium .... An agricultural people originating in southeastern Europe is believed to have spoken a language that scholars consider the original Indo-European.

1st millennium .... The Germanic-speaking peoples separate out of the Indo-European group.

A.D.

5th–7th centuries .... The groups known as the Angles, Saxons, and Jutes make incursions and, ultimately, settlements in the British Isles.

Late 7th century .... Foundation of monasteries in Northumbria in northern England. Period of Northumbrian religious and cultural efflorescence. Age of Caedmon and Bede.

Late 9th century .... Reign of King Alfred (871–899). Establishment of West Saxon hegemony over Anglo-Saxon England and the foundation of schools and scriptoria for the teaching and writing of Old English. Translations of classic Latin texts into the vernacular.

Late 10th–early 11th centuries ..... Period of Benedictine monastic revival in Anglo-Saxon England. Production of sermons in Old English by Bishop Aelfric and others. Teaching done in English and Latin in Anglo-Saxon schools.

c. 1000 .... Date of the *Beowulf* manuscript, text of the earliest major long poem in English.

1066 .... Norman Conquest. Invasion of England by Norman French-speaking noblemen and soldiers.

1087 .... Death of William the Conqueror.

1154 .... Date of last entry in the *Peterborough Chronicle*, thus ending the sustained writing of Old English prose in England.

c. 1200 .... Probable composition of earliest poetry in Middle English (e.g., "The Owl and the Nightingale," Layamon's *Brut*, short lyrics).

1258 .... Proclamation of Henry III, first official text in English since the conquest (but the English is actually a translation of the French original).

1362 .... Parliament is addressed for the first time in English (but records are still kept in French).

1380s .... John Wycliffe supervises translation of the Bible into Middle English.

c. 1400 .... Death of Chaucer.

1417 .... Royal clerks use English for official writing.

1422 .... London Brewer's Guild adopts English as its official language by formal action.

1423 .... Parliament's records kept virtually all in English.

c. 1440s–1550s .... The Great Vowel Shift takes place, changing permanently the pronunciation of long stressed vowels in English and, as a consequence, determining the sound of modern spoken English.

1474–1475	William Caxton begins printing books in England.
1490	Caxton's *Eneydos*. In his preface, he reflects on language change and dialect variation in England.
1526	Publication, in Geneva, of William Tyndale's English translation of the Bible.
1607	Jamestown colony established in Virginia.
1609	Publication (unauthorized) of Shakespeare's *Sonnets*.
1611	Publication of the King James Bible.
1616	Death of Shakespeare.
1619	Alexander Gil's *Logonomia Anglica* is published. Reflects on changes in English and the importation of new words from North America.
1620	Pilgrims land at Plymouth.
1624	First Folio edition of Shakespeare's works.
1644	The English seize New Amsterdam from the Dutch and rename it New York.
mid-17th century	Colonization of South Africa by English and Dutch settlers.
1736	N. Bailey's *Dictionary* is published, culminating a century of responses to the importation and coining of new words in the language.

1747	Samuel Johnson publishes *The Plan of a Dictionary*, setting out his goals for lexicography in English.
1755	Samuel Johnson publishes the first edition of his *Dictionary*, in two volumes. It quickly becomes the defining work for language use and dictionary-making in England and America.
1761	Joseph Priestley publishes the first edition of the *Rudiments of English Grammar*.
1762	Robert Lowth publishes the first edition of the *Principles of English Grammar*.
1781	John Witherspoon coins the term "Americanism" in his writings on the English language in America.
1783	Noah Webster publishes the first edition of his *Grammatical Institute of the English Language*.
late 18th century	Settlement of Australia by released and escaped convicts from penal colonies.
1799	Sir William Jones delivers his third-anniversary address to the Asiatic Society in Calcutta, announcing his discovery of similarities among the Sanskrit, Greek, Latin, Germanic, and Celtic languages, thus inaugurating the study of Indo-European.
1822	Jakob Grimm publishes the revised edition of his comparative grammar of the Germanic languages, codifying the consonant

relationships of the Germanic and non-Germanic Indo-European languages. This set of relationships came to be known as Grimm's Law.

1828 .... Noah Webster publishes the first edition of his *American Dictionary*.

1851 .... Publication of the first edition of Melville's *Moby Dick* (as *Moby-Dick*).

1855 .... Publication of the first edition of Walt Whitman's *Leaves of Grass*.

1857 .... Great Mutiny in India; establishment of direct imperial rule in India.

1863 .... Lincoln's Gettysburg Address.

1881 .... Publication of the first volume of Joel Chandler Harris's "Uncle Remus" stories.

1883 .... Publication of Mark Twain's *Adventures of Huckleberry Finn*.

1886 .... First publication of *Hobson-Jobson*, a guide to Anglo-Indian English.

1888–1933 .... Publication of the *Oxford English Dictionary*, originally called the *New English Dictionary* to distinguish it from Johnson's.

1905 .... Publication of Otto Jespersen's *The Growth and Structure of the English Language*.

1919 .... First edition of H. L. Mencken's *The American Language*.

1921 .... Publication of Edward Sapir's *Language*.

Glossary

alliteration: The repetition of the initial consonant or vowel of words in sequence. Old English and Old Germanic poetry was alliterative in structure: The metricality of the poetic line was determined not by the number of syllables, rhyme, or classical metre but by the number of alliterative words in stressed positions.

analogy: The process by which certain grammatically or morphologically different words or expressions come to share the same form or pronunciation.

analytic language: A language in which grammatical relationships among words in a sentence are determined by the order of the words in that sentence.

anaphora: A term used in rhetoric to describe the repetition of a word or phrase, usually at the beginning of successive sentences or clauses.

Anglo-Saxons: The Germanic peoples who settled the British Isles beginning in the 5th and 6th centuries A.D. and who spoke Old English. Conquered by the Normans in 1066, they were gradually absorbed into the Norman French-speaking population.

argot: A distinctive way of writing or speaking, often characterized by a unique vocabulary used by a particular class, profession, or social group.

articulatory phonetics: The study of how sounds are produced in the mouth, and the technique of accurately describing those sounds by using special symbols.

aureate diction: Use of an elaborate Latinate vocabulary used by English writers of the 15th and 16th centuries to evoke a rarefied and highly "educated" tone in their language.

back vowels: Continuous sounds produced at the back of the mouth (see **front vowels**, **high vowels**).

calque: A bit-by-bit, or morpheme-by-morpheme, translation of one word in one language into another word in another language, often used to avoid bringing new or loan words into the translating language (e.g., Modern German *Fernseher* is a calque on *television*;

Afrikaans *apartheid* is a calque on *segregation*; the modern Icelandic *moðorsik* is a calque on *hysterical*).

Chancery English: The form of the English language developed in written documents of the 15th century in Chancery (the official writing center of royal administration). Many grammatical forms and spelling conventions of Chancery English have become part of standard written English.

cognate: Two or more words from two or more different but related languages that share a common root or original.

comparative philology: The study of different but related languages in their historical contexts, traditionally with the goal of reconstructing earlier, lost forms of words and sounds in the Indo-European languages.

creole: A new language that develops out of the sustained contact among two or more languages. Often, creoles develop when the language of a colonizing or economically dominant group is imposed upon a subordinate or colonized group. Thus, many creoles have elements of both European and non-European languages. Creoles may emerge over time from pidgins. The basic difference is that creoles are perceived by the language speakers as the natural or native language, whereas pidgins are perceived as artificial or ad hoc arrangements for communication (see **pidgin**).

deep structure: In the linguistic theory of Noam Chomsky and his followers, the mental or genetically encoded pattern of language communication in human beings (see **surface structure**; **transformational-generative grammar**).

descriptivism: The belief that the study of language should describe the linguistic behavior of a group of speakers or writers at a given moment and should not be pressed into the service of prescribing how people should write or speak (see **prescriptivism**).

determinative compounding: The process by which new nouns are created in a language by yoking together two normally independent nouns (e.g., *earring*). A key feature of the Germanic languages, especially Old English, it is the process by which many poetic compounds were formed in literature (e.g., Old English *banlocan*, is *bone locker*, or body).

dialect: A variant form of a language, usually defined by region, class, or socioeconomic group and distinguished by its pronunciation, vocabulary, and on occasion, morphology.

dialectology: The study of different regional variations of a given language, spoken or written at a given time.

diphthongs: Vowel sounds that are made up of two distinct sounds joined together (e.g., the sound in the Modern English word *house*).

etymology: The systematic study of word origins, roots, and changes. The etymology of a given word is its history, traced back through its various pronunciations and semantic shifts, until its earliest recorded or reconstructed root. A root is also known as an *etymon*.

extension in function: The increase in the range of grammatical functions that a given word carries over time.

extension in lexis: The increase in the range of meanings, often figurative, that a given word carries over time.

eye dialect: A way of representing in writing regional or dialect variations by spelling words in nonstandard ways. Spellings such as *sez* or *wanna* are eye dialect forms; they do not actually record distinctions of speech but, rather, evoke the flavor of nonstandard language.

front vowels: Continuous sounds produced at the front of the mouth (see **back vowels, high vowels**).

grammar: Generally used to refer to the system of establishing verbal relationships in a given language; often confused with standards of "good usage" or "educated" speech.

grammatical gender: The system by which nouns in a language carry special endings or require distinctive pronoun, adjective, and article forms. Described as masculine, feminine, and neuter.

Great Vowel Shift: The systematic shift in the pronunciation of stressed, long vowels in English, which occurred from the middle of the 15th century to the middle of the 16th century in England and permanently changed the pronunciation of the English language. It effectively marks the shift from Middle English to Modern English.

Grimm's Law: A set of relationships among the consonants of the Germanic and non-Germanic Indo-European languages, first codified and published by Jakob Grimm in 1822.

high vowels: Continuous sounds produced at the top of the mouth (see **front vowels, back vowels**).

homonymy: The state in which two or more words of different origin and meaning come to be pronounced in the same way.

Indo-European: The term used to describe the related languages of Europe, India, and Iran, which are believed to have descended from a common tongue spoken in roughly the 3rd millennium B.C. by an agricultural peoples originating in southeastern Europe. English is a member of the Germanic branch of the Indo-European languages.

inkhorn terms: Words from Latin or Romance languages, often polysyllabic and of arcane scientific or aesthetic resonance, coined and introduced into English in the 16th and 17th centuries.

lexicography: The practice of making dictionaries.

lexis: The vocabulary resources of a given language.

metathesis: The reversing of two sounds in a sequence, occasionally a case of mispronunciation but also occasionally a historical change in pronunciation.

Middle English: The language, in its various dialects, spoken by the inhabitants of England from roughly the period following the Norman Conquest (the late 11th century) until roughly the period of completion of the Great Vowel Shift (the early 16th century).

modal verbs: Helping verbs, such as *shall*, *will*, *ought*, and the like, that were originally full verbs in Old and Middle English and became reduced to their helping function in the 16th and 17th centuries.

Modern English: The language, in its various dialects, that emerged after the end of the Great Vowel Shift, roughly in the middle of the 16th century.

monophthongs: Vowel sounds that are made up of only one continuously produced sound (e.g., the sound in the Modern English word *feet*).

morpheme: A set of one or more sounds in a language that, taken together, make up a unique, meaningful part of a word (e.g., "-ly" is the morpheme indicating manner of action, as in *quickly* or *slowly*; "-s" is a morpheme indicating plurality, as in *dogs*).

morphology: The study of the forms of words that determine relationships of meaning in a sentence in a given language. Includes such issues as case endings in nouns, formation of tenses in verbs, and so on.

Old English: The language, or group of related dialects, spoken by the Anglo-Saxon people in England from the earliest recorded documents (late 7th century) until roughly the end of the 11th century.

periphrastic: A term that refers to a roundabout way of doing something; used in grammar to describe a phrase or idiom that uses new words or more words than necessary to express grammatical relationship.

philology: The study of language generally but now often restricted to the historical study of changes in phonology, morphology, grammar, and lexis. Comparative philology is the term used to describe the method of comparing surviving forms of words from related languages to reconstruct older, lost forms.

phoneme: An individual sound that, in contrast with other sounds, contributes to the set of meaningful sounds in a given language. A phoneme is not simply a sound but, rather, a sound that is meaningful (e.g., "b" and "p" are phonemes in English because their difference determines two different meaningful words: *bit* and *pit*, for example).

phonetics: The study of the pronunciation of sounds of a given language by speakers of that language.

phonology: The study of the system of sounds of a given language.

pidgin: A language that develops to allow two mutually unintelligible groups of speakers to communicate. Pidgins are often ad hoc forms of communication, and they are perceived as artificial by both sets of speakers. Over time, a pidgin may develop into a creole (see **creole**).

polysemy: The state in which one word comes to connote several, often very different, meanings.

©2008 The Teaching Company.

prescriptivism: The belief that the study of language should lead to certain prescriptions or rules of advice for speaking and writing (see **descriptivism**).

regionalism: An expression in a given language that is unique to a given geographical area and is not characteristic of the language as a whole.

semantic change: The change in the meaning of a word over time.

slang: A colloquial form of expression in a language, usually relying on words or phrases drawn from popular culture, particular professions, or the idioms of particular groups (defined, for example, by age or class).

sociolinguistics: The study of the place of language in society, often centering on distinctions of class, regional dialect, race, and gender in communities of speakers and writers.

strong verb: In the Germanic languages, a verb that indicates change in tense by changing the root vowel: e.g., *think, thought; drink, drank, drunk; bring, brought; run, ran* (see **weak verb**).

structural linguistics: The discipline of studying language in America in the first half of the 20th century, characterized by close attention to the sounds of languages, by a rigorous empirical methodology, and by awareness of the marked differences in the structures of languages. The term is often used to characterize the work of Edward Sapir and Leonard Bloomfield.

surface structure: In the linguistic theory of Noam Chomsky and his followers, the actual forms of a given language, uttered by speakers of that language, that are produced by the rules of that language and are generated out of the deep structures innate in the minds of humans.

syntax: The way in which a language arranges its words to make well-formed or grammatical utterances.

synthetic language: A language in which grammatical relationships among words in a sentence are determined by the inflections (for example, case endings) added to the words.

transformational-generative grammar: The theory of language developed by Noam Chomsky and his followers which argues that all human beings have the ability to speak a language and that deep-structure patterns of communication are transformed, or generated, into surface structures of a given language by a set of rules unique to each language. Presumes that language ability is an innate idea in humans (see **deep structure, surface structure**).

weak verb: In the Germanic languages, a verb that indicates change in tense by adding a suffix, usually in "-ed": e.g., *walk, walked; love, loved* (see **strong verb**).

Biographical Notes

Alfred, King of England (849–899). King of the Anglo-Saxons (r. 871–899). Consolidated West Saxon political hegemony in southern England; commissioned the translation of major Latin works into Old English; provided the political aegis for the establishment of the West Saxon dialect of Old English as a standard.

Bede the Venerable (c. 673–735). Anglo-Saxon monk, historian, and grammarian. Best known for his *Ecclesiastical History of the English Church and People*, in which he records the poetry of Caedmon, the first known poet in the English vernacular.

Bibbesworth, Walter of (b. in or before 1219–d. in or after 1270). Thirteenth-century writer of a treatise on French for English aristocrats and gentry.

Bloomfield, Leonard (1887–1949). American linguist and author of *Language* (1933), a highly influential text in the American school of structural linguistics (stressing empirical observation of spoken language).

Caedmon (fl. late 7th century). First known poet in English; wrote a hymn about creation in Old English that was considered to be the first English poem.

Caxton, William (c. 1421–1491). England's first printer. Brought printing to England in the 1470s and published for the first time the works of Chaucer and many other important English writers. In the prefaces to his works, he reflected on language change and variation.

Chaucer, Geoffrey (c. 1340–1400). Major English poet of the 14th century. Wrote *The Canterbury Tales* and other poems in Middle English.

Chomsky, Noam (1928–). American linguist. Revolutionized the study of language and the discipline of linguistics with the publication of his *Syntactic Structures* (1957) and other books. Founded the approach known as transformational generative grammar.

Douglass, Frederick (c. 1817–1895). African-American writer and politician of the 19th century. Wrote several autobiographical works that describe his experiences as a slave and record the varieties of African-American English of his time.

Gil, Alexander (1564–1635). English schoolmaster and grammarian; master of St. Paul's School in London; teacher of Milton. Published several works on the English language in which he responds to issues of spelling reform and the increase in the language's vocabulary (notably, *Logonomia Anglica*, 1619).

Grimm, Jakob (1785–1863) and **Wilhelm** (1786–1859). German linguists, lexicographers, and folklorists. Collected stories of the German people into well-known volumes of fairy tales; produced the major historical dictionary of the German language. Jakob Grimm formulated the sound relationships for Indo-European languages that have come to be known as Grimm's Law.

Harris, Joel Chandler (1848–1908). American writer and folklorist. Best known for his "Uncle Remus" stories, which seek to record the speech and literary forms of African-Americans of the late 19th century.

Jefferson, Thomas (1743–1826). Third president of the United States; author of the Declaration of Independence; student of the history of the English language (especially Old English). His writings influenced the rhetoric of American public discourse throughout the late 18th and 19th centuries.

Jespersen, Otto (1860–1943). Danish linguist. Wrote extensively on the history and structure of the English language, in particular in his influential *Growth and Structure of the English Language* (1905).

Johnson, Samuel (1709–1784). English writer, poet, and lexicographer. His *Dictionary* (1755) set the standards for lexicography for more than a century.

Jones, Sir William (1746–1794). English diplomat and philologist. His recognition that the languages of Europe and India share certain key features of grammar and vocabulary led to the development of Indo-European comparative philology in the 19th century.

Lowth, Robert (1710–1787). English scholar, bishop of London, and author of several influential books on English grammar. Advocate of prescriptivism in the study of language.

Mencken, H. L. (1880–1956). American journalist and critic. Best known for his cultural criticism and for his book *The American Language* (first published in 1919, then reissued with supplements and revisions over the following 30 years).

Mulcaster, Richard (c. 1530–1611). English schoolmaster and grammarian. Head of Merchant Taylors' School in London (where Edmund Spenser was a student); later head of St. Paul's School. Wrote about English grammar and usage, recording many features of 16th-century English.

Müller, Max (1823–1900). German-born philologist, professor of linguistics and Oriental languages at Oxford, and arbiter of scholarship in historical linguistics in mid-19th-century Europe.

Murray, J. A. H. (1837–1915). English lexicographer and primary editor of the *Oxford English Dictionary* from 1879 until his death.

Priestley, Joseph (1733–1804). English clergyman, scientist, and grammarian. Published several books on English grammar. Advocated a primarily descriptivist approach to the study of language.

Sapir, Edward (1884–1939). American linguist and anthropologist. Major contributor to the American school of descriptive, or structural, linguistics, especially through his work with Native American languages.

Shakespeare, William (1564–1616). English dramatist and poet. In his plays and sonnets, he deployed the resources of a changing English language of his day to give voice to character, theme, and dramatic setting.

Twain, Mark (Samuel Clemens, 1835–1910). American writer, best known for his novels of mid-19th-century life on and around the Mississippi River, especially *Huckleberry Finn* (1883), and his social satires, especially *A Connecticut Yankee in King Arthur's Court* (1889). In his writings, he often recorded or sought to evoke the regional dialects of his characters.

Webster, Noah (1758–1843). American lexicographer and educator. His early spelling books of the 1780s were immensely influential on schoolroom education, and his *American Dictionary* of 1828 became the standard reference work for spelling and pronunciation in the United States.

Whorf, Benjamin Lee (1897–1941). American linguist and anthropologist, best known for the view that the language of a speech community shapes its perceptions of the world.

William the Conqueror (c. 1027–1087). First Norman French king of England. The Norman Conquest (1066) initiated the cultural and linguistic changes that eventually helped transform Old English into Middle English.

Witherspoon, John (1723–1794). Scottish-born American clergyman; signer of the Declaration of Independence; president of Princeton University. Wrote extensively on the American version of English; coined the term "Americanism."

Bibliography

Aarsleff, Hans. *The Study of Language in England, 1780–1860.* Princeton: Princeton University Press, 1966. Still the best account of the philosophical and cultural fascination with language in the 18th and early 19th centuries and the best "prehistory" of the *Oxford English Dictionary.*

Algeo, John, ed. *The Cambridge History of the English Language,* Volume 6: *English in North America.* Cambridge: Cambridge University Press, 2002. The new standard in advanced scholarship in the study of English in North America.

———, *Problems in the Origins and Development of the English Language.* San Diego: Harcourt, Brace, Jovanovich, 1972. A textbook guide with exercises on the history of the language.

Barnet, Sylvan, gen. ed. *The Complete Signet Classic Shakespeare.* San Diego: Harcourt, Brace, Jovanovich, 1972. A good classroom-level edition of Shakespeare.

Barney, Stephen A. *Word-Hoard: An Introduction to Old English Vocabulary.* New Haven: Yale University Press, 1977. A clever interpretive lexicon of Old English literary terms.

Baugh, Albert C., and Thomas Cable. *A History of the English Language.* 5th ed. Englewood Cliffs: Prentice Hall, 2004. The standard history of the language in textbook form.

Bennett, J. A. W., and G. V. Smithers. *Early Middle English Verse and Prose.* Oxford: Oxford University Press, 1968. An excellent anthology with full annotations and a glossary.

Benson, Larry D., ed. *The Riverside Edition of the Works of Geoffrey Chaucer.* Boston: Houghton Mifflin, 1987. The standard scholarly edition of Chaucer's works.

Benveniste, Emile. *Indo-European Language and Society.* Trans. Elizabeth Palmer. Miami: University of Miami Press, 1973. A brilliant and original work of cultural history through linguistics.

Bertram, Paul, and Bernice W. Kliman, eds. *The Three-Text Hamlet.* New York: AMS Press, 1991. The three texts of *Hamlet,* ranged in parallel.

Blake, Norman, ed. *The Cambridge History of the English Language,* Volume 2: *1066–1476.* Cambridge: Cambridge

University Press, 1999. The new standard in advanced scholarship on Middle English.

————. *The English Language and Medieval Literature*. London: Methuen, 1979. A wide-ranging account of medieval English literature in its linguistic context.

Bloomfield, Leonard. *Language*. New York: Henry Holt, 1933. The defining work of the structural linguistics school.

Bolton, W. F. *A Living Language: The History and Structure of English*. New York: Random House, 1982. A provocative, idiosyncratic textbook history of the language.

Bryson, Bill. *The Mother Tongue: English and How It Got That Way*. New York: Avon Books, 1991. A lively, conversational history of the language by one of our best travel writers and journalists.

Burgess, Anthony. *A Mouthful of Air: Language and Languages*. London: Hutchinson, 1992. An imaginative encounter with English and its history, by one of the most inventive novelists of the 20th century.

Cannon, Christopher. *The Making of Chaucer's English*. Cambridge: Cambridge University Press, 1999. A landmark scholarly study of Chaucer's use of Middle English vocabulary.

Cassidy, F. G., and Richard Ringler. *Bright's Old English Grammar and Reader*. 3rd ed. New York: Holt Rinehart Winston, 1971. A comprehensive textbook to Old English.

Cassidy, Frederic, chief ed. *Dictionary of American Regional English*. Cambridge: Harvard University Press, 1985. The new standard dictionary of American Regional English.

Chomsky, Noam. *Aspects of the Theory of Syntax*. Cambridge: MIT Press, 1964. The first synthesis of Chomskyan linguistic theory; a field-defining work.

————. *Syntactic Structures*. The Hague: Mouton, 1957. Chomsky's landmark monograph that changed the field of linguistics.

Clanchy, M. T. *From Memory to Written Record*. 2nd ed. Oxford: Blackwell, 1993. A groundbreaking study of the place of literacy in medieval English life.

Clark, Cecily, ed. *Peterborough Chronicle*. Oxford: Oxford University Press, 1970. The standard scholarly edition of an important Late Old English prose document.

Cohen, Murray. *Sensible Words: Linguistic Practice in England, 1640–1785*. Baltimore: Johns Hopkins University Press, 1976. A scholarly study of early theories of language and the beginnings of English linguistics.

Crystal, David. *The Stories of English*. London: Allen Lane, 2004. A lively account of the history of the language by Britain's leading historian of English.

Culler, Jonathan. *Ferdinand de Saussure*. 2nd ed. Ithaca: Cornell University Press, 1986. A clear, deft introduction to the work of the founder of modern linguistic study.

Darnell, Regna. *Edward Sapir*. Berkeley: University of California Press, 1990. A well-written study of the life and work of one of the founders of structural linguistics.

DeMaria, Robert. *Johnson's Dictionary and the Language of Learning*. Chapel Hill: University of North Carolina Press, 1986. A scholarly account of the making of Johnson's dictionary.

Dillard, J. L. *Black English*. New York: Random House, 1972. A good, if now somewhat dated, survey of African-American English.

Dobson, E. J. *English Pronunciation, 1500–1700*. 2 vols. Oxford: Oxford University Press, 1968. A full, detailed, yet idiosyncratic survey of the so-called "orthoepists" and the Renaissance study of language.

Douglass, Frederick. *Autobiographies*. New York: Bonanza Books, 1972. A convenient edition of the personal writings of the great 19th-century African-American writer.

Dowling, Linda. "Victorian Oxford and the Science of Language." *Publications of the Modern Language Association of America* 97 (1982): 160–178. A scholarly article detailing the historical environment in which the *Oxford English Dictionary* took shape.

Fisher, John H., *The Emergence of Standard English*. Lexington: University of Kentucky Press, 1999. A collection of scholarly essays by a leading scholar of Early Modern English.

———, et al. *An Anthology of Chancery English*. Knoxville: University of Tennessee Press, 1984. An important collection of original documents of 15th-century English.

Fishkin, Shelley Fisher. *Was Huck Black? Mark Twain and African-American Voices*. New York: Oxford University Press, 1993. A provocative, if at times overstated, account of Twain's sources for Huckleberry Finn's language.

Fliegelman, Jay. *Declaring Independence*. Stanford: Stanford University Press, 1993. A brilliant, imaginative study of the making of the Declaration of Independence and the early American culture of rhetoric.

Gates, Henry Louis, Jr. *The Signifying Monkey*. New York: Oxford University Press, 1988. The major work of African-American literary theory.

Giancarlo, Matthew. "The Rise and Fall of the Great Vowel Shift?" *Representations* 76 (2001). A scholarly article exploring the ways in which 19th- and 20th-century philologists came up with the idea and the evidence for the Great Vowel Shift.

Godden, Malcolm. "Literary Language." In Richard M. Hogg, ed., *The Cambridge History of the English Language*, Vol. 1: *The Beginnings to 1066*, 490–535. Cambridge: Cambridge University Press, 1992–2002.

Himan, Charlton, ed. *The Norton Facsimile: The First Folio of Shakespeare*. New York: Norton, 1958. A facsimile edition of the first major volume of Shakespeare's works.

Hogg, Richard M., ed. *The Cambridge History of the English Language*. 6 vols. Cambridge: Cambridge University Press, 1992–2002. The complete scholarly standard set of volumes: English from its origins to the present day; from Britain to the world.

Jones, Gavin. *Strange Talk: The Politics of Dialect Literature in Gilded Age America*. Berkeley: University of California Press, 1999. A brilliant critical account of the role of dialect in the making of 19th-century American literature.

Kachru, Braj. *The Indianization of English*. Oxford: Oxford University Press, 1983. A good scholarly account of the relationships among Indian and English languages and their cultural contact.

Kermode, Frank. *Shakespeare's Language*. London: Allen Lane, 2000. A personal account of Shakespeare's English by one of Britain's leading literary critics.

Labov, William. *The Atlas of North American English*. www.ling.upenn. edu/phonoatlas. The great work of dialectology by America's leading descriptive linguist.

Lass, Roger. "Phonology and Morphology." In Roger Lass, ed., *The Cambridge History of the English Language*, Volume 3: *1476–1776*. Cambridge: Cambridge University Press, 1999. An important scholarly survey of the forms and sounds of Early Modern English.

Lawton, David. "Englishing the Bible." In David Wallace, ed., *The Cambridge History of Medieval English Literature*. Cambridge: Cambridge University Press, 1999. A provocative history of the traditions of Bible translation into English.

Lerer, Seth. "Hello, Dude: Philology, Performance, and Technology in Mark Twain's *Connecticut Yankee*." *American Literary History* 15. A scholarly article about Mark Twain's uses of philology in his *Connecticut Yankee*.

—. *Inventing English: A Portable History of the Language*. New York: Columbia University Press, 2007. A personal history of the language, keyed to individual moments in its development.

—. "Old English and Its Afterlife." In David Wallace, ed., *The Cambridge History of Medieval English Literature*. Cambridge: Cambridge University Press, 1999. A scholarly account of the end of Old English and the beginning of Middle English.

—. *The Yale Companion to Chaucer*. New Haven: Yale University Press, 2006. A collection of essays on Chaucer by the leading scholars of the early 21st century.

Mack, Ruth. "The Historicity of Johnson's Lexicographer." *Representations* 76 (2001). A scholarly article about the ways in which Johnson's personality emerges from his dictionary.

Marckwardt, Albert H. *American English*. Revised, J. L. Dillard. Oxford: Oxford University Press, 1980. A good scholarly survey of the major lines of development of American English.

Marcus, Leah. *Unediting the Renaissance*. London: Routledge, 1996. A provocative argument for reading Renaissance English literature in its original forms.

Marvin, Carolyn. *When Old Technologies Were New*. New York: Oxford University Press, 1988. An excellent history of the 19th-century inventions of the telephone and other electrical devices.

McCrum, Robert, William Cran, and Robert MacNeil. *The Story of English*. New York: Viking, 1986. The illustrated, well-written companion book to the popular PBS series of 1986.

Melville, Herman. *Moby Dick*. Harmondsworth: Penguin, 1976. A great paperback edition, rich with historical and cultural annotations.

Mencken, H. L. *The American Language*. 4th ed., abridged and revised. New York: Alfred Knopf, 1977. A lively, idiosyncratic history of American English in all its forms.

Milroy, James. "Middle English Dialectology." In Norman Blake, ed., *The Cambridge History of the English Language*, Volume 2: *1066–1476*, pp. 156–206. Cambridge: Cambridge University Press, 1992. A complete scholarly survey of Middle English dialects.

Mossé, Fernand. *A Handbook of Middle English*. Baltimore: Johns Hopkins University Press, 1968. A scholarly introduction, grammar, and collection of texts for the study of Middle English.

Mufwene, Salikoko S. "African-American English: Structure, History, and Use." In John Algeo, ed., *The Cambridge History of the English Language*, Volume 6: *English in North America*. Cambridge: Cambridge University Press, 2001. A complete scholarly survey of African-American English.

Mugglestone, Lynda. *Lost for Words: The Hidden History of the OED*. New Haven: Yale University Press, 2005. A fascinating account of how the *Oxford English Dictionary* was put together, by the leading historian of the dictionary today.

Murray, J. A. H., et al., eds. *The Oxford English Dictionary*. Oxford: Oxford University Press, 1933. The great historical dictionary of the language.

Murray, K. M. Elisabeth. *Caught in the Web of Words: James A. H. Murray and the Oxford English Dictionary*. New Haven: Yale University Press, 1977. A learned yet affectionate account of the origins of the *Oxford English Dictionary*, by the founding editor's granddaughter.

Nevalainen, Terttu. "Early Modern English Lexis and Semantics." In Roger Lass, ed., *The Cambridge History of the English Language*, Volume 3: *1476–1776*. Cambridge: Cambridge University Press, 2000. A full scholarly account of the vocabulary changes in Early Modern English.

Newmeyer, Frederick. *The Politics of Linguistics*. Chicago: University of Chicago Press, 1986. A provocative set of arguments about the intersections of politics and language study in late-20th-century America.

Nunberg, Geoffrey. *The Way We Talk Now: Commentaries on Language and Culture* from NPR's "Fresh Air." Boston: Houghton Mifflin, 2001. Radio essays from our leading cultural commentator on language.

O'Keeffe, Katherine O'Brien. *Visible Song: Traditional Literacy in Old English Verse*. Cambridge: Cambridge University Press, 1990. A brilliant scholarly assessment of the relationships of literacy and poetry in Anglo-Saxon England.

Orgel, Stephen, and A. R. Braunmiller. *The Pelican Shakespeare*. Harmondsworth: Penguin, 2002. An excellent new classroom edition of Shakespeare.

Pyles, Thomas. *The Origins and Development of the English Language*. San Diego: Harcourt, Brace, Jovanovich, 1971. A solid textbook history of the language.

Reddick, Alan. *The Making of Johnson's Dictionary*. Revised ed. Cambridge: Cambridge University Press, 1996. A full scholarly account of just how Johnson put his dictionary together.

Renfrew, Colin. *Archaeology and Language: The Puzzle of Indo-European Origins*. London: Jonathan Cape, 1987. A brilliant anthropological account of the early culture of Indo-European peoples, by the leading British anthropologist of early Europe.

Rickford, John Russell and Russell John Rickford. *Spoken Soul: The Story of Black English*. New York: John Wiley & Sons, 2000.

Rissanen, Matti. "Syntax." In Roger Lass, ed., *The Cambridge History of the English Language*, Volume 3: *1476–1776*. Cambridge: Cambridge University Press, 2000. A detailed, scholarly account of changes in syntax in the Early Modern English period.

Samuels, M. L. *Linguistic Evolution, with Special Reference to English*. Cambridge: Cambridge University Press, 1972. A provocative, original account of theoretical problems in why language changes and how English changed.

Sapir, Edward. *Language*. New York: Harcourt Brace and Co., 1921. An important, defining work in the development of structural linguistics in America.

Steiner, George. *After Babel: Aspects of Language and Translation*. New York: Oxford University Press, 1975. A lively personal account of problems of translation in culture and literature.

Stenton, F. M. *Anglo-Saxon England*. Oxford: Oxford University Press, 1971. A standard history of England before the Norman Conquest.

Strang, B. M. H. *A History of English*. London: Methuen, 1970. A brilliant if unusual "reverse" history of the English language—from present to past.

Traugott, Elizabeth Closs, and Mary Louise Pratt. *Linguistics for Students of Literature*. San Diego: Harcourt Brace Jovanovich, 1980. A good introduction to Chomskyan linguistics and its impact on reading literature.

Turville-Petre, Thorlac. *England the Nation: Language, Literature, and National Identity, 1290–1340*. Oxford: Oxford University Press, 1996. A readable, scholarly engagement with the trilingual culture of medieval England.

Uitti, Karl D. *Linguistics and Literary Theory*. New York: W.W. Norton, 1974. A good introduction to the relationships between Chomsky's work on linguistics and the study of literature.

Watkins, Calvert. *The American Heritage Dictionary of Indo-European Roots*. Boston: Houghton Mifflin, 1985. An engaging, learned introduction to the study of Indo-European linguistics and the place of Indo-European in our modern languages.

Webster, Noah. *An American Dictionary of the English Language*. Facsimile reprint. Anaheim: Foundation for Christian Education, 1967. A facsimile of the great American dictionary.

Whorf, Benjamin Lee. *Language, Thought, and Reality*. Cambridge: MIT Press, 1956. The collected papers of an original American linguist and theoretician.

Wills, Garry. *Lincoln at Gettysburg: The Words That Remade America*. New York: Simon and Schuster, 1992. An illuminating analysis of Lincoln's address by a leading journalist and popular historian.

Wimsatt, W. K. *Philosophic Words: A Study of Style and Meaning in the Rambler and Dictionary of Samuel Johnson*. New Haven: Yale University Press, 1948. An old but still useful study of Johnson's key vocabulary terms in his criticism and lexicography.

Yule, Henry, and A. C. Burnell. *Hobson-Jobson: A Glossary of Anglo-Indian Words*. William Crooke, ed.; new foreword by

Anthony Burgess. London: Routledge and Kegan Paul, 1985. A reprinting of the great dictionary of Indian English.

Notes